HEART of the LION

Talks given at the Sahaj Marg Seminar
April 9 - 25, 1993
in Lenasia, South Africa.

by
Shri Parthasarathi Rajagopalachari
President
Shri Ram Chandra Mission

First Edition: October, 1993   2,000 Copies

All rights reserved

©Shri Ram Chandra Mission
North American Publishing Committee
Molena, GA, USA, 1993

No part of this book may be reproduced in any form or by any means without permission in writing from Shri Ram Chandra Mission.

Printed in U.S.A.

ISBN 0-945242-24-7

HEART *of the* LION

Shri P. Rajagopalachariji

Contents

I.	The Friend	1
II.	Nothingness	21
III.	Pain	57
IV.	The Purpose of Existence	71
V.	Dedication of Lenasia Ashram Site	91
VI.	Pitfalls of Spirituality	95
VII.	Love Thy Neighbour As Thyself	117
VIII.	The Beauty of the Heart	147
IX.	A Child's Wonder	171

The Friend
April 10, 1993

This morning, in the bedroom which Rassikbhai has given to me, I saw a photograph which brought back old memories — Babuji Maharaj washing his hands in the wash basin near his bedroom. A very important thing happened in my life right at that wash basin. Perhaps I have spoken about it before. One morning at four o'clock Babuji wanted to go to the toilet, so I took him to the toilet. All night I had been trying to remember it, but I had forgotten his name! And then I thought his Master's name was the same name, so if I remembered that, I should remember his name, but also that name I could not remember. So I was very upset. I thought there had been some fall at night, some loss of spiritual values, spiritual state — *haalat* as we say in Hindi. So when I took him to the bathroom and brought him back he was washing his hands, and in the mirror he looked at me and said, "You look worried. Why?" I said, "Babuji, there is something wrong with me!" He said, "Four o'clock in the morning, how can anything be wrong?" I said, "Yes but, you know, how to tell you? I am ashamed I cannot remember your name, and I cannot remember your guru's name, because I thought if I remembered his name, your name is the same, I would automatically remember." You know, with his beard wet, with his hands wet, he embraced me and he said, "Wonderful!" "*Mubarak ho!*", he said in Hindi. "Congratulations." He said, "This is the real condition. That you do not know your guru's name is the best condition." I said,

"How can that be?" He said, "The guru really has no name. He has assumed a name for you to be able to call him, for instance." He cannot say, "Hey you!" like the American does. Nobody will turn back and say, "Are you thinking of me?" He's not going to look back and say, "Are you calling me?" He has no form. It is another assumption, or what he has assumed so that we can recognize him.

No name, no form — he has no qualities. You cannot call him, "You, kind man, please come to me." Is he kind? I have often said, "Not at all." Of course there are many devotees here who will probably take up a Zulu spear to throw at me! *Assegaai!* But I suppose I can have *mukabala* (confrontation) with that too, if necessary. It's not a difficult thing. But to say "Master is kind," is a wrong thing. Is he cruel? Of course not, because one who is not kind is not necessarily cruel. See, it is a human fallacy to only deal with opposites. "He is not rich, so he must be poor. He is not white, therefore he must be black. He is not a man, therefore he must be a woman." How can he be a woman? It's, I mean, something wrong with grammar or with facts.

So we are always going to extremes in our appreciation of values, of life. "The food is not good, therefore it must be bad. It is not tasty, therefore it must be distasteful." But we forget that reality lies between the opposites. It is neither this, nor that. To my understanding, you know, which matured over the years — it is still maturing, one can never know the Master. Obviously when he has no name, when he has no form, when, as I found, he has no qualities, no attributes — how can you ever know him? Then what is the way of finding out this mysterious thing called the Master? Babuji Maharaj said, "You cannot know God, but you can experience God." So a Master is a matter of experience. Not of acceptance or denial, not of knowing or unknowing, not of having or not having, not of calling or not calling, not of welcoming or not welcoming, but of experiencing.

I wonder how many of you experienced anything yesterday at the airport, because all the way from Mauritius, even though I was talking to these people on the plane, I was transmitting to all those abhyasis of South Africa, also transmitting to those at the airport, and bringing them together in the airport finally and transmitting to them there. How many of you felt it? See now, there is a bit of psychology involved in this. Those of you who think of Him, in whatever way it is, will feel something. Those of you who refuse to think of Him in one way, but only in another way, may not feel Him, or His transmission. Those of you who negate will not feel anything at all.

So what is this business of acceptance? You see, it is like a wife. When you marry, you accept, "This is my wife." Then she is everything to you. As the Veda says, finally she is your mother! She has to be your wife, she has to be your beloved, she has to be your lover, she has to be your cook, she has to be everything. A man is only one thing to a woman, but a woman is everything to a man. *Ekadasham kruti*, says the old Veda. At the time of marriage, when the woman is blessed, and the couple is blessed, the Vedic mantra says, "Give him eleven children, and make him your twelfth child!" Of course by then the man is generally senile, toothless, and he very much needs a mother! That is when a man misses his woman the most. You know, it is the old man who misses his wife more than the young. The young man only misses her in bed. He misses his fun, he misses his pleasure. The old man misses his wife. The young man doesn't miss his wife. He misses his sex, his pleasure, his fun. He misses good cooking, he misses pressed clothes, well washed. But when you are old you miss your wife. Like good wine which matures, human relationships must mature. Oh, when a young man, you know, says "I miss my wife," he doesn't know what he's really missing. Or perhaps he knows but he is trying to hide it in different language. "I am missing my wife." When an old man says "I miss my wife," it is something very total in concept. That is why old people, when their wives die, they die very soon sometimes. You know, in the animal world, in the bird world, the mate does not last much longer. Of course, many human beings try to find a second wife! But really, a wife cannot be replaced. You can replace a sexual partner, you can replace a romantic partner, you can replace a cook. If your wife has been merely a cook, you can change her with not much difficulty, you see, with not much difference. If she has only been a concubine to you, you can buy them by the dozen. But if she has been a wife to you, well you are going to lose one half of your existence.

Now if this is the case only with a wife, with a mere wife, what is it with a Master? But a Master is not to be experienced as a sense object. Babuji Maharaj defined the world once, perhaps in Germany, if I remember right. Somebody asked the question, "What is the world?" He said "Sensed object." We know the world only through our senses. We see it, we touch it, we smell it, we taste it, we enjoy it. So it is a sensory world. Is it real? Obviously not. That which is merely sensory, which responds only to my senses, which gratifies only my senses — how can it be real?

So you see, when we die, are we losing this world, are we leaving this world? It would be stupid to think, "Oh, I am leaving this world behind, this beautiful world I have seen, full of so many beautiful things," and becoming desolate about it, sad about it, miserable about it, afraid of the next life. How can it be the fact? Material things are transitory things. Today here, tomorrow not here — even the world, even the universe!

The old Vedic wisdom speaks of the universe being destroyed and recreated perpetually, eternally. It speaks of the ultimate Lord, you see, who is reclined in ultimate *samadhi*. With the outgoing breath He creates a world. With the indrawing breath He destroys it and takes it back into Himself, which you call the *mahapralaya*. Just a breath of the Lord, and it is measured in spans of time which are staggering, so you cannot even put it in words, you cannot even write it in figures. Four million, three hundred thousand years is supposed to be *kali-yuga*. Forty three million years was the preceding. Four hundred and thirty million years, the previous one, and four thousand, three hundred million years, the first *yuga*, the *treta-yuga*. Add up these, and you get a staggering figure. In between each *yuga* there is a *sandhi*, and that is four million, three hundred thousand years long. Like you have the dawn and the dusk which unite the day and the night at either end, you have the *sandhi* between *yugas*, and when you total this up it is one *maha-yuga* only. And the Manu is supposed to be living for so many *maha-yugas*.

That is why in the Indian concept of time, you start with the second, the minute, the hour, then the dark half of the day, the bright half of the day, the dark half of the fortnight, the bright half of the fortnight, the *paksha*, as you call *shukla paksha, Krishna paksha*, then the dark half of the year, and the bright half of the year, the *ayana*. The sun's motion towards the north and the sun's motion towards the south. The *daks-ayana* and the *utar-ayana*. And one year is but a day in the life of even a person like Indra, of the Pitras, and they live a hundred such years, and a hundred such years lives the deva, and a hundred of those years lives Indra, and Brahma lives for so many *kalpas*. And the Veda says even Brahma has to come down here. Even Vishnu has to come down. Even Shiva has to come down to this *karmabhumi* and live as a human being again, and work their way into the spiritual evolution.

So don't look for long life. Brahma is going to live for many *kalpas*, but he is not long-lived, he is short-lived. You know, Ravana is supposed to have lived for, I don't know, a hundred thousand years, or something like that, and the story goes, you know, that Brahma was washing his hands, and somebody went to him and said, "Ravana has just been born." He said, "Oh, I see," and by the time he finished his tooth brushing they came back and said, "Ravana is dead. Killed by Rama." He said, "*Alpayush* — short-lived blighter! By the time I brushed my teeth he has already been born and dead!" So people who seek long life are stupid because Brahma has to come back here, and Brahma is jealous of human beings because we have an opportunity which he doesn't have. He has to rule his kingdom from wherever he is and cannot be liberated from there. He has to come back here.

So you see, the sensory world is a trap. Beautiful things — glitter, romance, glamour. No harm, it is also Nature's creation, but — not to be attached. Ice cream? Well good, why not? If it is given with love, eat it, but don't think of it a second time. Don't ask for a second one, don't think of it at night before going to bed and say, "Oh, I wish I had an ice cream now!"

You know, there are many vulgar stories I have heard which illustrate these truths beautifully, but I cannot say them

The Friend

in the presence of women, unfortunately. One woman asked me in Denmark, "Do you differentiate between man and woman? You are a *chela* of Babuji Maharaj." I said, "Etiquette makes me differentiate! I don't. I mean, I am as capable as any drunkard of talking body things in public, but etiquette forbids." She said, "How to hear these stories from you?" I said, "Become a man!" (laughter) "Then perhaps I will be able to tell you these stories." But there are very, you know, really fascinating stories if you are willing to understand the meaning of those stories, it is something really, you know, out of the Vedas, I should say. After all, even the Vedas speaks, you know, when the human being asks his guru, "What is this *ananda* that you are talking of?" You know, it comes in the Taitraiyi Upanishad. He says, "What is this *ananda* you are speaking of?" You know, he starts by defining life. He says "This is the *ananda* of the mind, this is the *ananda* of so and so ...," ultimately he says, "*Manusha ananda,*" and the definition is — the pleasure that you have in sexual intercourse. See, this is the definition given in the Vedas, and the Vedas are not body texts. "Why?", I asked, you know, my guru of those days, who was a Sanskrit pandit. He said, "Because in this single thing, all the five senses are put together." Beauty, wonderful perfume, soft and sweet words, silky touch, taste — I suppose there must be something in kissing! — unless it's lipstick!

So you see, the five senses come together — *pancha indriya*. Therefore it is so powerful, therefore it is almost impossible to overcome its pull. Because of the strength of this pull, its enormous pull, which is Nature. Nature has created this potency because for its purpose it wants procreation to continue so that life can evolve. Procreation is not meant for our pleasure, but to give an opportunity for souls to be reborn which have to be reborn, so that they may go on their onward path towards the spiritual goal. Therefore in Hinduism we have this concept that marriage is a must — that a man must have children, because if you stop with your education, you are not a teacher, but when you start teaching you become a teacher. What I have learned I must pass on. What I have become I must pass on. If I have this enormous benefit, which even Brahma does not have, of being born as a human being, I must pass on this benefit through my, you know, life itself, and create fresh life, giving an opportunity to other souls to be reborn in this human form.

This is the idea of procreation in Hindu tradition. This is the idea of marriage. Therefore, in the Hindu concept marriage is holy, sex is holy, procreation is holy, but only in the right way. So you see when a man and a woman united in marriage, united in love, unite physically, it is with the idea that, "Lord, let there be a blessed child." You know, even rishis who have not had children have prayed to Lord Shiva. A thousand years, and Shiva finally comes and says, "Well, what do you want?" "I want a *putra*." You know there is a *yagna* called *putra kameshti yagna*, and Shiva says, "Yes, I can give you a wonderful child who will die at the age sixteen, or you can have one who will live hundreds of years, see his grandchildren and great-grandchildren. Which do you want?" In their foolishness, or perhaps in their wisdom, they say, "We want the wonderful child, even if it only lives sixteen years." Because when you have no children, a child is a blessed thing, and a child living sixteen years — well sixteen years is a long time. So you think, but as this child ages the day is coming nearer and nearer and the parents become sadder and sadder, and you know what happened — the story of Markandeya.

The Friend

So you see, a child is a divine blessing, not to be aborted, not to be contracepted, not to be thrown on the rubbish heap. Therefore, spiritual wisdom says, "Beware how you procreate, with whom you procreate." Is the vessel fit to receive the seed? You don't go and put, for instance, your cabbage on a heap of cow dung — you won't eat it afterwards. Would you? You select the soil, you select the seed, and you tend that growth with love. Not to eat the fruit, but to see the beauty of that which is growing, and to rejoice in that beauty and to rejoice in a small way in your part in being a creator for the moment. Therefore, it is also said in the Veda that it is in the sex act that a man approaches nearest to the Creator, because he is creating life himself. But if it is for fun, if it is for pleasure, if it is out of a moment of temptation, it cannot be Brahmahood that we enjoy for the moment — it is lust!

So you see, spiritual values are only giving an attitudinal change, a change of direction to the very same thing that we are doing all the time. The purpose is different, the attitude is different, the attitude with which we approach it is different. It does not mean that a saint has no wife, or he doesn't sleep with her. Babuji had six children. In fact, one man in, I think, France or Denmark, he said, "Oh, if he had so many children, Chariji, he must have really enjoyed his sex!" I said, "I never asked him that question. It would not have been good etiquette to ask my Master, 'Babuji, did you enjoy sex?'" But why not? You see, he was living in a body. Rama had children (Luva and Kusha), Krishna had children. Who did not have children? But the way they had the children, and the children they had — that is what we have to judge. Did he produce a monster? Or did he produce children who could stand up to the father and say, "What did you do with your wife? Where is Vaidehi?"

Heart of the Lion

You know, Rama was going to do one of those famous *yagnas* after Sita had passed off, and he had made a *putli* of gold, a figure of gold of Sita sitting next to him, and he was going with the *yagna*. In the Vedic tradition, no man has a right to perform any sacred *yagna* without his *dharma-patni* by his side. The word *dharma-patni* is very significant, because there can be *adharma-patnis* — *patnis* of the moment. Bought *patnis*, willing *patnis*. *Dharma-patnis* is one who is the wife in the way of *dharma* — upholding life. *Dharma* means the support, the base.

So not every romance is with a wife, or a concubine. The law may award it but spirituality does not. You see, the famous court scene with Portia — the law allows it, the court awards it! But in marriage there is no law, there is no court, there is only the moral law. Because, I think it was our friend, our sister here, who said, "Some speakers are very moralistic." We have to be moralistic in times of immorality, in times of grossness, in times of decadence. We have to go to hospitals when we are sick, and if the doctor says, "No smoking, no drinking, no sex," you have to abide by it. "Oh, he's a moralistic doctor. He doesn't want me to have any fun in life. I'll change my doctor." Well, it's time for you to telephone your undertaker and, you know, reserve your plot! You should reserve your plot for your burial well in advance. Beware of a doctor who says, "Oh yes, why not? But, keep it down!" "Three times a day, doctor?" "Well, perhaps, why not, but two might be better, one best!" One what? He doesn't know.

So beware of a guru also who tells you, "Yes, why not?" Can he make black money? "I will give fifty percent to the Mission." "Yes, yes! Make crores!" Such a guru is not trustworthy. The guru who says you can have fun with your

The Friend

women is not trustworthy. A guru who says you can cheat in business is not worthy of being your guru. A guru who says, "What is there — it is all life." You know, I was traveling once to Balsar in a first class compartment. I was smoking. There was a sannyasi outside in his usual yellow robes surrounded by, you know, I could recognize some of them — the top cinema stars, directors, cameramen — hundreds of them. I was hoping that he would sit in a third class compartment, but he walked into my compartment and sat next to me. So immediately I threw down the cigarette and stamped on it. He said, "*Nay, nay, piyo* — smoke!" I said, "But Swamiji, how can I smoke in your presence?" He said, "This is also created by God!" (laughter) I said, "Swamiji, that's a very convenient philosophy." He said, "My son, God is a convenience that we have created for ourselves. God creates everything. I don't think God will frown at a little pleasure." Then I understood why all these cinema stars and, you know, movie directors were around him! (laughter)

So you see, yesterday we were talking about friendship, friendliness, friendly attitude, God reality. I must tell you one rather *kaduva* truth: The Guru is the only friend you will ever have. I repeat — He is the only friend you will ever have. If you understand the significance of the proverb or the old way of saying who is a friend: a friend in need is a friend indeed. When do I need a friend? When I am in trouble, when I am in difficulties. A man who is well off and enjoying his life, he doesn't need friends. Of course, he is surrounded by so-called friends who are hypocrites who want to share in his prosperity, in his fun, and because he doesn't like to be alone he is surrounded by these sycophants, he throws his money around and they enjoy. No. A friend in need is a friend indeed. If you are in need, how many of those whom you call your friends will come to you? Sometimes I wish there should be a moment of disaster in every man's life, because that is the moment when you will be helped to find out who are your true friends. In prosperity, in good health, when you are at the peak of your name, fame, and fortune, you are always wondering, "Who is my real friend?" When a man is in power in politics, he does not know who are his friends. It is at the time of fall, when we are sick, when we are miserable, when we are alone, that we can say, "Here is the friend who comes," you see, and only one person will come to you then.

Such a person must have the right to criticize you, to curse you, to kick you if necessary. If you do not give him that right, don't ask for his friendship, because if he is your true friend he has to help you, he has to give his life for you. He cannot do it unless you permit him to do it. If you say, "No, no, what is this — this blighter is always calling me names, criticizing me, telling me not to smoke, telling me to get rid of six out of my seven girlfriends and marry the seventh one... I don't want! I can find friends enough." Yes. They will not aid you — they will give you AIDS! Many acts of aid does not make AIDS. AIDS is not the plural of aid.

This is a stern warning I must issue to all of you. A really stern warning — that if you are not fit to be kicked around, or not willing to be kicked around, don't go for spirituality. Find one of these false gurus, spurious gurus. You know, there are many cults, many organizations where they will praise you, and while they are praising you and hugging you they will take the purse out of your pocket as beautifully as one of the light-fingered gentry can do it. You won't even know that you have lost a crore of rupees. All that you will get in return is your name on a piece of marble outside their temple. Donors — list of donors, starting with the biggest, ending with the smallest. How long will it last? As long as

The Friend

the temple lasts. How long is the temple going to last? Well, nothing created by man lasts forever.

So you see, a friend need not be friendly. Remember this. It is only in material things that honey must be sweet, lime juice must be *khattah*, you know, *khattah, mitta*, all this nonsense. Yes, because in nature there is no change. A mango is always a mango. I would love to have a mango which will taste sour to me because it's not good for me, and I would throw it away and say, "No, no," and the mango says, "Sensible fellow! I will come back to you sweet when you can tolerate it, when I am good for you." That is also the role of the wife. The wife must learn to say no to her husband. What is the disaster that has taken over the Occidental world in their love, in their marriage situations? The inability of the woman to say no. I hold the women squarely responsible for degeneration — moral degeneration — anywhere, in any society, white or black, Hindu or Muslim — anywhere. Where a woman cannot say no, that society is plunging towards disaster. I have said this in the white countries — they were very angry with me. I now say it in our countries here, with black and brown people. They will also be angry with me, but the woman knows in her heart that when she cannot say no, she is slipping. Not sleeping, as some Gujaratis would say, but slipping.

To say no is the most difficult thing, and like a wife, a guru must know when to say no. If he cannot say no, he is useless. If a guru is always saying "Yes, yes," "Can I go out for half an hour and see the beauty of this country?" "Yes, why not!", shun him. "Can I have a little whisky? Just a little?" "Yes, yes. It's good." You know yesterday I was reading an article in the magazine on the plane, where it says a little wine a day keeps the heart attack away! So come to your guru and say, "Babuji, can I have a little drink? You know, my heart!" "Your heart?", Babuji was very innocent. "What do you mean, my heart?" "No, no, you know, this heart," patting your chest, and then Babuji quietly looks at somebody sitting near him and says, "I wonder whether this fellow has a heart at all!"

Make sure you have a heart. We all imagine we have hearts — golden hearts, spiritual hearts. Make sure you have a heart, not just a pump, pumping away futilely. Make sure you have the heart, then start developing that heart into something into which divinity can plunge itself and renew itself and come out, you know, as you.

So I repeat, the Guru is the only friend. In fact, I have said this so often, that in the Sufi philosophy the guru is called Friend. They say, "The Friend is coming." Because he is the only fellow who can give his life for you. He is the only fellow therefore to whom you must hand over totally a power of attorney — "Do with me as you think I deserve to be done, as I deserve to be done with. Kick me when I have to be kicked. Beat me when I have to be beaten. Curse me when I have to be cursed. But make of me what you think I should be eventually, because only you can do it."

So, once more I say this in all humility — if you must have a Master, find a fellow who is capable of, you know, throwing you around, beating you up, cutting you to pieces. Remember Parushurama's father and the stern test that young boy had to make for obedience — "Kill your mother." "Yes." He pulled out his sword and cut off her head. He said, "I am pleased with you, my son. Ask for anything you want." He said, "I want my mother alive." And he said, "So be it," and she got up and walked off. The Guru is the Guru is the Master, when you say of destiny, it means of life and death. He

The Friend

must be the master of your life as he must be the master of your death.

If the Master does not come to me in my final moment when I shall close my eyes for the last time, it is useless, because that is when I need him most, because that is when I take my step through a door that has never been open so far in my existence and I don't know what lies beyond. I may be stepping off a precipice and falling to my ultimate death. Who knows, when I open that door, what is going to happen to me. Then the Master comes and says, "Come." He takes the hand and leads you lovingly to your goal. But he can do that only if throughout your life you have given him the charge over yourself, kept your hand in his, like a trusting child with its hand in its mother's hand, and gone where he goes. Trusting him, loving him, knowing that he will not do anything against your interests because, after all, his interest in you can never be less than your interest in him. His goal for you can never be less than the goals you have set for yourself. His love of life, your life, can never be less than your own love of your own life. If you have understood these things with your heart, then you will never withdraw your hand from him. Even if he wants to shake it loose, you will not allow it to be done.

Therefore, Babuji said, "Look for such a one who can lead you to your goal, and having found him, bind him to yourself with chains of steel." Why? They should be unbreakable. Even in a moment of anger, of temper, of renunciation, so-called, we should not have the ability to break the chain that we have tied around him and us. What about his strength to break it? Of course he can break anything. But he doesn't come to us to throw us off, or to shun us, or to repudiate us, or to break the chain that we have forged with him. The danger is always that we shall break the bond. Therefore we have to tie, with chains of steel, the Master and ourselves together, because in a moment of despair, in a moment of anger, in a moment of weakness, the abhyasi should not be tempted to cut the chain and run away. Only slaves cut chains. Only prisoners break doors and escape. Devotees, never.

So I pray that all of you should have these senses awakened in you — the real senses — the sense of what is good for me, the sense of who is good for me, the sense of what is a friend, who is a friend — not of friendliness. The true friend, the Guru, has no need to be courteous, no need to be polite, no need to have etiquette towards you in his behaviour. We are translating into the spiritual world merely, what shall I say, values of etiquette and politeness that we practice in human intercourse. "Is he a human being?" Of course! "He is my friend, can I address him as friend?" Well, decide in your heart how you can address him. In our Hindu culture, the husband can call his wife by name, but the wife cannot call her husband by name. "Hey, Ramu *yavo!*" What do you think of such a woman? "Oh, I don't think they're married, sir. No Indian woman would call her husband by name." Today it is the fashion. It is taken as the sign of equality of the sexes. A cheap equality in which you can call your husband by name, and you think you are a woman? Shame. You have lost much in gaining very little. "*Ranjit aavo.*" "*Arre kaun bulaveche mane.*" "Mama mia, my wife is calling me by name. I don't know what is happening in this household." It is crazy, it is artificial, it is stupid.

So let us hold onto our Hindu culture very tightly. Let us not sacrifice the ideals of womanhood, especially in India. You know, in India a woman is something very great. Don't

The Friend

be misled by what these Occidentals tell you, that a woman should not walk three paces behind her husband — are you not equal, should you not, you know, put your arm around his waist and walk like we walk? "Look at us. La-la-la-la, we are going walking." And tomorrow morning the girl is missing or the man is missing. Where is that arm around my waist? Gone with the wind, gone forever, like two pictures I saw in my childhood.

These cultural values are the bastion which protects us. They are the values which nourish us, which make us enriched in our life. That which enriches must be protected. You can leave cow dung on the heap, but you don't put vitamin pills on cow dung; they are in bottles. The Hindu way of life is a supremely benevolent and good way of life. Let us not barter it away for flippant ideals such as women's lib. The woman is no more free than the man when they are married. The man enjoys an apparent freedom because he can go to work, he flies around earning his money, so a woman thinks, "Oh, you know, he can go anywhere he likes." He does not go anywhere he likes. He goes to see his customers, he goes to collect his money, he goes to see his suppliers. They are not everywhere, everywhere. He cannot go to Mauritius for a holiday. Which businessman takes a holiday? The richer they are, the less of holidays they have. Isn't it? So let not our women be foolish and think, "Oh, my man can go where he likes. He can go in the morning at six, come back at ten at night." For your sake! He is slaving for you, for your children that you have borne to him. Don't you think he should do it? Or should he lead a happy life wandering around the gardens of Johannesburg singing around trees? That is a false world of romance which doesn't exist. You know how many times they say a man hasn't married, and yet how many affairs they have. In and out of affairs, and it is very symptomatic of the truth of what they say, that the French call it "*l'affaire de coeur*" — an affair of the heart. I call it "*l'affaire de corps,*" given my own broken knowledge of French. I hope it's an improvement!

So, cherished values, values which have lasted centuries, values which keep the beloved protected, cherished, nourished, let not the beloved throw away. It is not freedom to break these cultural ties — they are not bonds. When young plants are growing we put protective devices around them so that the cows may not graze on them. We send our children to school with somebody else, so that they are not abducted on the way, kidnapped on the way. We live in houses with doors and windows precisely for protection. Protection should not be confused with imprisonment. In prison you are not under protection. I hope nobody thinks that a prison is a place where we are protected. Only some of the Mafia dons prefer to be in prison, because then their enemies cannot shoot them down. But even there they penetrate, and Mafia dons have been shot in prisons. There is no protection in prison. It is where society is protected from you.

So you see, coming back to this idea of friendship — don't expect friendliness from your only friend. From your other friends, yes, they should be friendly, they should be polite, they should praise your *dokla* even when it has no salt — doesn't matter. "*Saruche*." But with the Friend, remember that he is the only one who will stand by you through thick and thin, through adversity, through prosperity and pain, through suffering. And however he may behave, whatever he may say, accept it as something in your good, for your good, for the ultimate destiny of ultimate release from existence itself. Thank you.

Nothingness

April 11, 1993, Morning

We often speak about the Master, and how his capacity is nearly divine, if not divine. Babuji Maharaj said so many times that God has no mind. That is a specialty of Sahaj Marg philosophy. In our own experience of life we also know that God is heartless. I mean, it doesn't need any explanation. In the Occident people are always asking, you know, "According to many religions and philosophies, it is said God is love. So if he is love, how does he allow little children to be born incapacitated, babies having AIDS, children being born blind, children being tortured, children being abducted and raped?" — all this, you know, the whole panoply of inhuman civilisation that we have had after half a million years of so-called human existence, perhaps a million years of human existence.

If you look at today's human beings, one may perhaps be tempted to say that over these million years of evolution to what we call *homo sapiens* today, the animal in man seems to manifest itself more and more. Of course, the primitive underdeveloped societies are always blamed. I see here, in the South African press, this tendency to blame one section of the population over the other, to say that they are crude, they are dirty, they are filthy, they are primitive, they are animals, etc. But I don't think the other half is any less animal, I only think they have whitewashed it, tailored it a nice suit, given shoes to it, and cosmetics. Smells nice, but it is still as violent and as animal as the other half.

Heart of the Lion

There is a saying in India that, "To clap you need two hands." One hand cannot clap. So similarly, for violence to exist there must be two sections of society, and it's a moot point, a debatable point, as to which is responsible. It is like a couple where the two partners to the couple blame each other for all their mess.

So, coming back to this idea that more and more animal tendencies are being manifested as our greed, our avariciousness grows in a materialistic environment, we know for a fact, you see, that God has no heart. We know from the teachings of the Master that God has no mind. Then what is this Divine capacity we are talking about? So I have ventured to suggest that the Divine only creates. When I asked Babuji Maharaj, "Why does the Divine create?" He said if He did not create — excuse the masculine gender for God, but that is our traditional way of looking at God — we cannot say "the chairperson" — God is not the chairperson. He is very much the chairman, and this is not a matter of male chauvinism, it is a philosophy in itself. When I asked Babuji why He creates, he said, "He would suffer from power grossness if He didn't." He has to create. Then what happens is, in this creation of ours we have all the raw materials necessary for evolution, and we as human beings, we have been blessed — sometimes I think we have been cursed — with an intelligence and the will power to guide our own destinies — one helping us to choose the right destiny, the other giving us the power, the motivating power to go on that path, the chosen path.

So what I am trying to suggest is that there is no use looking to a God to correct us, or our societies, of our tendencies. The buck stops here, and the **here** is — each man pointing to his own heart, each woman pointing her finger to

Nothingness

her own heart — towards yourself. The buck stops here. So now we have to wonder, you see, what is this role that the Master is going to play in this. Has he any role at all? Can he help us? Of course, it is almost a truism, it doesn't need an explanation, that help can only be forthcoming if my direction is right. Obviously, if I am going towards Capetown and somebody is going towards Zimbabwe, he cannot give me a lift! It's obvious, and there is no use ranting and raving and saying, "Oh, these blighters, they are going all the time towards Zimbabwe when I want to go south towards Capetown. Why doesn't somebody help me? Where is this God you are talking so much about?" Babuji can help only in an established direction in which he can take us, and in no other.

This has to be very definitely understood, then it will avoid a lot of disappointment. It will obviate the need to curse the Master roundly whenever we feel like it. It will also remove our foolishness and childishness in expecting the Master to pamper us, to fulfil our every whim, our every pleasure, and decide once and for all that he is a spiritual guide who can guide me on my spiritual destiny, offering of course such palliatives as I may need on the journey. There is nothing against his helping me materially if he chooses to do it, but that is not his job. After all, if I am a passenger on a train and I have forgotten my water bottle, there is no law which says that another co-passenger will not give me a sip from his bottle, or a sandwich from the basket of another person, but they are incidental. They are not planned, and we should not depend on that. We have to equip ourselves in all possible ways to undertake this journey, this enormous distance we have to cover, which Babuji Maharaj says, nevertheless is no distance, covered in no time.

Heart of the Lion

So do we really need all this paraphernalia that we put together when we go on a journey? Not if you are going to take it as a journey of no time and no space; very much yes, if you are thinking of it as a long journey over a long stretch of time. It depends on you. If any one of us here has the capacity, has the gumption, has the spunk to say, "I shall leap into eternity here from now. All that I need is to jump. I don't need anything else." But if I want to walk down the precipice like a slow-moving ant, creeping here, creeping there, crawling around, afraid of falling, afraid of breaking my neck, holding on to the Master for dear life, or forgetting in the process thinking I can do it myself, and falling to my destruction — then of course I need parachutes, I need hang-gliders, I need helicopters above to rescue me in case of disaster — I need everything.

So we think of the Master in several ways. Some of us tend to think of him as a banker who will help us in our business, making us free of the problems of cash flows, etc. Some of us think of him as a supervisor of a health club, helping us to rejuvenate ourselves, to remain young, youthful. Some, as a sort of a marriage bureau, providing life partners, or not-so-long life partners! For the nonce! Some, as a ticket issuer, you see, who has only to give me the ticket to eternity and then fade out of the picture. "I don't need him any more. I have my ticket, why do I need the old fellow now? Doesn't make sense, Chari, to carry the travel agent with you to Bombay, does it?" Not at all.

So how we look upon the Master also is a very clear indication of what we are. Each one of you can decide for yourself what the Master is to you, and therefore what you are now in this moment on the spiritual journey. You don't have to look into your journals, you don't have to look into

Nothingness

your heart. Just think of what you think of your Master, and you know, it's like solving one of these mathematical equations — shift the equation around and you have the answer. If X is equal to Y, Y is equal to X! You don't even have to change the factors around.

So this fascinating problem of what is a Master, who is a Master, why a Master — it is entirely up to you to provide the answers. The Master is helpless, he has no answers, he cannot answer any of these questions except by one answer, saying, "You know it already." Babuji Maharaj used to be very polite. He was an extremely cultured person. He would say, "You are intelligent. You already know what the Master is." They went home satisfied, thinking that they were right in what they thought the Master was! Of course, they were partially right. The businessman went home thinking he is the banker, and when his loan didn't come through he said, "What have I got into? This man, you see, he even told me that I am right in what I think of as the Master. And yet no loan! How can it be possible?" So a long letter comes, "Babuji Maharaj, I have been dependent solely on you," and then poor Master says, "Now, what should I do? How to answer this letter?" Sometimes I have known him walking up and down in his house for three days, not knowing how to respond to a letter, because his etiquette forbade him to write the truth about the other man. About himself, there was no such thing as the truth to write, because he was all things at all times, and therefore something to someone at some times, and nothing to somebody at no time, everything to someone at all times. He was a whole, you know, spectrum of possibilities. So how could he say what he was, except in relation to a particular individual? Someone thought of him as God, someone thought of him as a beggar without education, someone thought of him as a silly, idiotic Hindu trying to ape Mahatma Gandhi.

Somebody said, "What is he when there is Aurobindo and Ramakrishna Paramahamsa and Rajneesh? This man, living in a pokey hole in a dirty lane in filthy Shahjahanpur — what is he?" And when you ask him, "What do you get from Rajneesh?", they say, "Oh, come on Chari, don't be so naive! You know what Rajneesh gives. By Jove, it's wonderful!" As I said yesterday — AIDS. "What does Satya Sai Baba give you, or somebody else give you?" "Well, you know that too. He does miracles! So, what does your Master give you?" I said, "Nothing." He said, "There you are!" I said, "Yes, but can you find somebody who gives you **nothing**? Have you ever found anybody who can give you nothing in a very real sense?" Then they are stymied. They don't know what I am talking about, they think, "Well, this disciple is as bad as his Master. Only thing, the other looks like a fool, behaves like a fool, is a fool. This man looks educated, behaves educated, but is still a fool! How can anybody give nothing, for heaven's sake?" I said, "Oh, in that case, why do you say Babuji gives you nothing? If he cannot give you nothing, then why do you blame him for giving you nothing, when he really gives you nothing?" So you put them in a sort of a loop, you know. An intellectual, logical loop in which they are trapped and you can walk away whistling, for your morning walk, and leave them with their head in their hands trying to figure out what I said. You are accusing him of giving you nothing, yet when I say he gives you nothing, you deny he cannot give it. Then why do you blame him for giving nothing when in fact he cannot give you nothing. At least he cannot give you the nothing except the nothing that you are getting. Now I will put you all in this mess of

Nothingness

thought! (laughter) Leave you to work it out, you see, figure it out.

Because, in Sahaj Marg, God is nothing. He is not a person, He is not a place, He is not a thing. He does not fulfil the classical definition of a noun. A noun is the name of a person, a place, or a thing. He has no location in space. He has no existence in time. He has no attributes. He is nothing. Now, who can give you that, except one who is a Master in giving you nothing?

Sahaj Marg is often made too simple by preceptors who want to make it easily available to abhyasis. It is easily available to abhyasis. It is easily practised, but when we are asked to assess what we have got, it is like an examiner with a blank sheet of paper in front of him from a genius who says, "Look there and you have the answer to this problem." It takes a genius to assess a blank sheet of paper. It takes a lover to read a letter in which there is only "My dear," and "Yours affectionately," at the other end. Some of you might have received such love letters. I don't know, I hope you have been fortunate enough. Where it is all written down, you know, it is limitation. "I love you." "Oh yes, of course, everybody says that!" At the same time you want to hear it, you are also suspicious because everybody says it. At the same time, everybody speaks the truth, but can the truth be spoken by everybody? Is it not lies which all people speak, only the truth some people say. Therefore, should my lover say, "I don't love you"? If he does so, would you be happy? So you see, this is another double-bind situation.

I am deliberately confusing you today, to break some of these cobwebs in your head — that Babuji was this, Babuji was that, Babuji was *extraordinaire*, and things like that. Babuji was nothing — this is my thesis. And being nothing, he could not give anything except nothing. And only those who want nothing from him should go to him and get that nothing! And if you are stupid enough to ask, "Why do I have to go to him to get nothing from him? Cannot I not get nothing at home?" Try it! If you can get nothing by sitting by yourself at home, you are a saint, you are almost divine yourself.

Therefore, this is the funny thing in Sahaj Marg, you see — that to get nothing I must want nothing. Wanting nothing, I must go to somebody who is nothing, who has nothing, and try to get from him the nothing that he has. It is an extraordinarily beautiful situation. It is a situation unparalleled in the history of human thought, in the history of human spiritual endeavour. Always people have gone to others for something. Never have people gone to somebody for nothing. For the first time in human history, we have an institution, we have a guide who says, "Come to me for nothing. I give you nothing. You take back nothing with you." And we are wondering, you see! And if you are able to wonder instead of feeling anger and frustration, you have begun your first step on the spiritual path.

This is really a wonder-full situation — a situation of wonder, a situation which can make us, each one of us, wonderful in our turn. Because when this nothingness has been received, we are nothing — yet full, complete. You know, it is like saying, a vacuumized vessel in a chemical plant, for instance — almost total vacuum, you see, but there is nothing in it. Yes, but look what happens when you open a single valve of that vacuum chamber. Everywhere else, when you open a valve things rush out. Here, when you open a valve, if the vacuum is powerful enough it can take in the whole universe into itself. Think of a black hole in space.

Nothingness

Think of a person who loves so much that nobody can stay away from that person. You are sucked into that, shall we say, orbit of influence of that love. You fall like insects, moths into the living flame. Only a lover wonders at the stupidity of a moth which immolates itself in a flame. He says, "For heaven's sake — committing suicide!" But if the moth could speak, it would laugh at us. "You are so near the light, and you are still alive? Are you not ashamed? What can you aspire to except this light, this living light, into which you must plunge and disappear forever in an act of ultimate union with that light? And you are holding yourself aloof, allowing it to illuminate your ugliness, your stupidity, your ignorance, your grossness, your avarice, your greed. Look at me, a humble moth — I cannot rest till I have totally burned in this flame."

Therefore Babuji wrote so much about the moth and the flame, going one step further and saying, "Any moth can immolate itself in a living flame, but rare is the moth which can immolate itself in a cold flame." Now we have to work that out, too. Where is this cold flame? How to find it? How to find the light which does not make itself visible to me? How, in fact, to find light without luminosity? Again this problem of something and nothing, or something appearing as nothing. Light appearing as darkness. Nothing appearing as something, or something appearing as nothing. Babuji giving, and we receiving, yet nothing being transferred from him to us. He feeding us, and we growing, but nothing actually going into our mouths!

So you see, this is a very, very paradoxical and difficult to understand *marg*, as we say in Hindi — a way. The easiest, perhaps, is to understand the Mission. It is his creation. It is an organization. It has a president at the top who has the dual function of the spiritual guide and the administrative head, assisted by a team of experts who constitute the working committee, and by a team of spiritual people called preceptors. Of course there is the usual paraphernalia of books and buildings and whatnot, without which an organization cannot exist as a service organization. We need these to serve. Don't make the mistake of thinking that the Mission builds ashrams for itself. It is like saying this building built itself for itself. It cannot build itself for itself. Somebody builds it for someone else to use. Even a businessman builds blocks and blocks of apartments to rent out for somebody's use — he doesn't stay in all of them. The Master is not in his ashrams.

Don't make the mistake of thinking that, "This ashram was charged for so many years — X,Y,Z, and therefore I don't need the Master any more — if I sit in that ashram I will get everything." It is like expecting your wife's photograph to make love to you! I mean, putting it very bluntly, you see. It may look even better than she ever did in her lifetime — most photographs do. Yet we can get nothing out of it except an image.

So the Mission is the easiest to understand precisely because it has the least part to play in our spiritual journey. It is a creation which he considered necessary to help us. We should allow it to help us in the way that he designed — meditate. Don't imagine that you can just sit in an ashram and become a saint. No ashram produced a saint, though saints lived in ashrams. Kings live in palaces, but if I went into a palace and lived there I wouldn't become a king!

Lamps give light, but just by sitting near a lamp I will not become a lamp. I must burn. I must allow myself to be burned, as Babuji Maharaj used the example of the candle. It consumes itself to illuminate everything. You cannot illuminate anything without consuming yourself. You cannot create love in others except by consuming yourself with that love, allowing yourself to be burned up in that love. People want today to get fulfilment in love. They want to **get** in love. They cannot. It is against the law of love, it is against the nature of love, it is against the divinity of love. One who loves has to give, not to take. It is impossible to take from it.

There is a beautiful image, you see, of light — light illuminates everything. We see everything in this universe only because of light illuminated, or light reflected, off the objects. But when the light reflects itself off the object, illuminating that object for us to see, it takes nothing from that object. It does not leave a single photon behind. It does not take a single photon from that object. It is reflected. Therefore this light can go on through eternity, proving in a perhaps unscientific but spiritual way that light is eternal. It goes round and round the universe. Einstein's theory, you see, that light can travel even through the deepest vacuums in space because it adds nothing to itself, it depletes nothing from itself, while illuminating the whole universe for us to see, for us to admire, for us to understand, for us to eventually overcome.

You must always understand one thing — that we need light only to avoid obstacles! If there were no obstacles we don't need light. When we walk in the darkness we carry a flashlight with us precisely to help us to see where there are obstacles and to avoid them. If I know that there are no obstacles in my path I can walk with my eyes blind, with my eyes blindfolded. I don't need vision. So you see, we are wondering about light, fascinated about light, employing the metaphor of light, yet knowing, or shall I say, not knowing that light is an unnecessary adjunct to our existence, needed only when we need it to show us where the obstacles are. And if I can remove those obstacles I can be totally in the dark. Paraphrasing Christ, perhaps we can say, "Blessed are they who don't see, for unto them is ensured a path on which there are no obstacles."

Babuji Maharaj said again and again that the greatest grossness is of the vision. Why do we meditate with our eyes closed? Many people have asked "Why can't I sit with eyes open and meditate?" Yes. Something in a miniskirt walks by and the meditation is gone! Or somebody brings a truckload of buns and wafers and ice cream — the other man's meditation is destroyed. Another one carries T-shirts and *salwar kamij*, and a third one's meditation is destroyed. So the eye is the most potent, shall we say, apparatus that we have for our guidance, and yet at the same time is potent with the possibility of degrading us, denigrating us, contributing to our fall. 'Close your eyes' is the first law of meditation. When the eyes are closed it becomes very easy to meditate.

So you see, really we don't need light for meditation. Often I am asked when I am to conduct satsangh, "Sir, should we leave the lights on in the hall?" I said, "Well, suit yourself. To me it matters not a whit. But can you sit in the light and meditate?" "No, no, we prefer dark." "Okay." You see, you actually come to state that you prefer the darkness to meditate in. Because the whole objective is to find that small sliver of light, a ray, perhaps, of light — like the ocean-going steamer looking for the lighthouse, the beam from the lighthouse to guide it to its port. In that darkness, in that immensity of our universal darkness, an internal universal darkness with which we are entombed in ourselves, all that I need is one ray of light from Him saying, "That is your destination."

Nothingness

This is the light that Babuji Maharaj said he created with the first sitting that he gave to an abhyasi. He said "I sow the seed of spirituality in the heart of the recipient." Then it is watered with his love, which is transmission. Now it becomes our duty to allow that light to grow. One does not light the lamp only to blow it out immediately. It must be allowed to grow and grow until the light not only fills our heart, but now flows out of us to illuminate everything outside us — now, each one of us can become the light.

When Christ said "I am the light and the way and the truth," what is the truth of existence? All this, you know, semantic understanding of truth, as that which is not the light, or that which states a fact — all this is philosophical blah blah, in the Occidental mode! Truth is the way of an existence dedicated to reaching the goal. He who is journeying towards the goal is going on the right way, the true way, the illuminated way. What is this way? It is but the Master who says, "I am also the way. I am also the truth. I am also the light. Follow me. Apart from me there is no other way. Don't look for Autobahn A-16!" And, "Thank you for bringing me up to this speedway or highway, Chari. Now I can go by myself. I have a map." Here there are no maps, because that which is at the other end of the universe for somebody, and yet is right in front of his nose to another person, cannot be mapped. "Is it not south, east, or west, or up or down?" It is everywhere for someone, it is nowhere for most people, it is right in my heart for somebody else. For such a person there is no guidance, no direction in which he has to move. He has to only go inside himself.

When you are in a swimming pool or outside a swimming pool, you don't think of jumping into it — which direction should you choose — should you come into it from the north or the east or the south or the west? You just dive into it. So this eternal swimming pool — it is a swimming pool, because Babuji Maharaj uses the words "swimming in the ocean of bliss". It is a swimming pool, which is a vast pool by any standards to those who are awe-struck by its immensity. It shrinks into nothing more than myself when I am confident that my Master is there. He has jumped in, I jump in, and I see that it is nothing at all — it is just a pool of water into which we went swimming. I am in it.

Does the ocean have a central point? Where is it? Does the galaxy have a central point? Yes. Technically, or shall we say, theoretically, there must be a point which is the centre of this galaxy of ours. But is it coterminous, shall we say, with the centre of this universe? Nobody knows where the universe begins, where it ends, where the centre of the universe is! So, which way shall I swim? And there comes the fascinating discovery that whichever way I may swim, if I am swimming with the Master, I am going towards the centre, because He is the centre.

One of the definitions of God, classical definitions, is that he is a circle with a centre everywhere and circumference nowhere. So, if this is a circle with its centre everywhere, should not the centre be here, too? Right here with us, right in each one of us? If you start thinking mathematically, using your intelligence and your education you will die a fool, because mathematics says one circle can have only one centre. Even a sphere can have only one centre. "What is this, Chari, you know, this is against the laws of mathematics." Okay, stick to your mathematics, become a professor, become a professor emeritus, build two, three houses, live happily, and I hope you will be reborn in your next life as not a mathematician at least! Because this way is not subject to any logic. It

Nothingness

is like asking a couple who have fallen in love, "For heaven's sake, how did you pick on this girl to love?" He can only say, "Well, with whom would you have fallen in love?" There is no explanation for love. There is no logic for love.

Why do you love your child? Why do you love your child more if it is retarded? Why do you kill yourself weeping for it, die for it? This is a fact of life. The father may not be there, but the mother — the more the child is disturbed, underdeveloped, the more she agonizes over it, prays for it, gives all her life to that child. What is the logic of love? "Oh, but Chari, don't you think we should love a nice handsome child who is growing well and, you know, growing in leaps and bounds towards a university education, ending up in Harvard, preferably?" That is a different logic, that is a materialistic logic, that is a selfish logic. Logic of love is unselfish.

Why does Master love us? Each one of us should have this, you know, this need to ask ourselves why the Master loves me, if I think he loves me? What am I that he should love me? We are ugly, we are stupid, we deny him at every possible turn. You all know how Christ predicted, at the Last Supper, that his best disciple Peter was going to betray him the next morning. "Before the cock crows twice thou shalt deny me thrice." And Peter was shocked. He said, "Me, deny you? It's not possible." But he did. The Master knows everything, you see, and because he knows everything, he understands us. He understands that we are gross. It is our grossness which makes us deny him. It is our grossness which makes us drunkards, womanizers, pilferers of money, and he says, "I cannot blame him or her, because he or she is not responsible. It is the grossness which is responsible." So, he can love us while hating our grossness. He can love us while cleaning us out. How many of us can love the toilets which we are cleaning, or the sewer which we are washing out? He loves even the sewer in us, precisely because he does not equate any of us with what we have inside ourselves.

We like a milk bottle, but if you put urine in it and ask somebody to carry it to the clinic for testing, how many of us would carry it without feeling a little, you know, "Oh my God, a urine bottle!" But the urine is inside, not outside, and if you don't know it, I will tell you an amusing joke about the rich man. My friend, who had called several people for a party — in the evening they had four bottles of whisky but they finished it in no time at all, and then they sent out for two more, and they were filled with urine. They were filled with urine and they drank it, not knowing it because they were too drunk! This is a real story, not a made-up one. And they paid 360 rupees for each bottle, and this was way back in 1962 — supposed to be this Black Dog, famous brand of whisky.

But Master does not deny us. He says, "Well, you are you; your grossness is something else. It is my problem. Leave it to me." But we are not willing to leave it to him. We say, "But Babuji, I feel so heavy, I feel light, I feel this, I feel that." And he says, "Look, I am telling you — forget yourself!" "Yes, but the Delphic oracle said 'Know thyself.' Yes, now what can I do? They were wise people who must have said it." "Now you may decide, you are intelligent." The ball is back in our court. One problem with my Master was, he never gave directions, he never gave instructions. He only nudged us in a certain direction, and if we did not accept it he would nudge us a second time, nudge us a third time, and then leave us to our destiny.

Nothingness

Recently I had one old preceptor from Babuji's times telling me that I am doing the Master's work as well as he did, but I am making a terrible mistake which Babuji never made. I said, "What is it?" He said, "You are running after abhyasis. You are too much with them. You are too much interested in their development. You are too much, you know, critical, and you are giving too much advice. They resent it. You should be like Babuji." I said, "How was Babuji?" He said, "But you know, Chari, he told them once, he told them twice, he told them a third time, not individually but in a group, and if they didn't accept it he just dropped them." I said, "But don't you think that is a dis-service?" He said, "Yes, if you think of it in one way, but then the Master cannot do dis-service to people." So I said, "Do you recommend that I should drop you if I nudge you three times in a given direction and you don't move in that direction?" He said, "For heaven's sake, don't do that!" (laughter) I said, "There you are. You want me to do that which you are recommending — Babuji never did — and suggesting that I should do, but you don't want me to do it in your case." I said, "I have a mandate from my Master. He said, 'All that I have not said because I could not say it — you have to say it. All that I could not do for various reasons — you have to do. If you have the integrity to do this, this Mission will shine as it has never shone in my lifetime. If you don't have it, it will decay. The Mission will fall into, you know, the limbo of lost things once again, perhaps to be resurrected after another ten thousand years by another Personality who shall come then.'"

When Babuji Maharaj said that such a Personality may not come for another ten thousand years, he did not mean that there is no Personality now on earth. He only meant if this Mission is lost, if this method is lost, as it was lost during the time of Raja Janaka, before him, seventy generations before him, it may take another seven hundred generations for it to be rediscovered. And like all lost things, it will end up in a lost property office where nobody goes to claim anything until, like the Customs in India, they start auctioning off all the confiscated goods and somebody goes and buys it.

So you see, we have to understand Sahaj Marg not with our minds, not with our intellect, not with our intelligence, not through the books, not even through the words of the Masters. Because the Masters are like the wind vanes — as the wind blows, it shifts its direction. There is nothing steady about the Master and his sayings. I can point out a thousand illustrations where Master has contradicted himself — apparently contradicted himself. I can tell you in my own life, someday you will read all about me in my diaries.

Incidentally, volume two of *In His Footsteps* has been published in the US. People in South Africa don't seem to be very keen on buying books. This is the land of gold and diamonds, I know. But books are more valuable. I suggest fifteen dollars for a book is not too high a price to pay, and since Santosh is here you should give your orders to him. It is rather, shall I say, depressing to find twenty copies of a book ordered with 300 abhyasis around, all of whom are wealthy enough to afford one or two books every year. That is by the side — you know I was a salesman all my life, I cannot stop selling things even now! The only thing I am not allowed to sell is spirituality, which we get free. But I do request you to buy books.

So you see, you can find contradictions in page after page after page. Only the fool looks for consistency. Consistency means a thing is fixed eternally. It cannot change, therefore it is a dead thing. The living truth, like the living river, must change course as it flows. You don't expect a river

Nothingness

to flow in a straight line, a geometrical straight line, down from its source to its destination on the ocean. It often goes against the very direction with which it started — oxbow lakes where part of it is stranded and has become a lake, going round in loops as if it doesn't know where it is going. But it knows very well where it is going, because the destination is pregnant in its presence. And it knows that to reach that destination it has to find the path which is going lower and lower all the time, never rising, and by sticking to the lowest path available it shall inevitably reach the ocean. Though, to our stupid eyes, to our geometrically trained eyes, to our logically trained minds, a river which could have been just two hundred feet long, is probably two miles long. So you see, again I repeat, logic — not mathematical logic, not physical logic, not chemical logic, no logic of any sort can apply to Sahaj Marg.

I remember C. Rajagopalachari, the last Governor General of India. He was accused of being inconsistent. He used to publish a newspaper called the *Swarajya*, a political newspaper in the times of Mahatma Gandhi. He often said things contraverting what he had said in a previous issue, and when he was questioned he said, "Consistency is the virtue of fools!" I recommend that for you, you see, because we are most of us living in foreign countries, and we have tended to become Westernized, Occidentalized. It's all right to wear a nice suit or jeans, but don't let your minds be influenced by this need for logic in everything that you do, in the need to understand the cause and effect sequence of what is happening, because Babuji Maharaj said, "There are causes without effects, there are effects without causes, and often the effect comes first and the cause later."

Heart of the Lion

Now, how to understand all this? If we think — Babuji was uneducated, eighth class, as he himself has said. You can say, "But Chari, he doesn't know anything! Eighth class man — how can he talk about logic? How can he talk about cause and effect? How can he talk about straight lines? What does he know of the universe?"

So we can have no assumptions about the Master. Every assumption is bound to be wrong. To assume he is God can be the greatest mistake we make. If possible, to assume that he is a mere human being may even be a greater mistake! Think over it. Don't understand, don't try to understand, don't worry about what he is — just understand with your heart what he can do for you. None of us have ever thought about salt, or its chemical composition, when we put salt in our food — enough that it is there. It makes my food palatable. Nobody thought of *hing*. What is *hing*? How many of you know where *hing* comes from? Some of you will say it is mined, some of you will say it's made in a chemical factory. It is only an exudation from a plant. And yet without *hing* there is no flavour! We are satisfied with the results. In Sahaj Marg, results are guaranteed to one who looks for results and does not try to examine the source of that beatitude which gives us all these results.

What does it matter to me where the Ganges originated, so long as it is flowing where I can have a bath in it, and where I can have water from it. Only fools will argue about that. Somebody says, "It was in the Himalayas," somebody says, "No, no, it was in Nepal," third man says, "It is in Bangladesh." How does it affect me? Does the water in my river change just because you think instead of Kathmandu it came from, I don't know, Johannesburg? What does it matter? What does the source matter? Enough that I have to go to

Nothingness

my destination. Even if my Master says, "The source is the destination," I don't have to know the source — I have only to know the destination. There I shall find out, perhaps by direct experience or direct perception, that the source was, is, and always will be the destination, but it does not mean I can go backwards in my journey to the source. I have to go forwards!

Now here comes another mystery, you see. "But the source, Chari — isn't it always behind me?" Are samskaras not created in the past? Does not a river begin in the mountains and go into the ocean? How can I go forward to reach the source? Well, try it. After all, the water in the ocean does evaporate, does go back as a cloud to the mountaintops, does furnish the water that flows down to you again. Leave it to the clouds to go back to the source and replenish it. You be happy with your destination. Perhaps you may also be vaporized. If I tell it to you in advance you may be frightened, you see, but without vaporization there is no third dimension movement possible to us. It is nice to sit in a high-flying plane, to look at those puffy white clouds, you know, outside, and imagine how nice it would be if I were a cloud like that. No visas, no plane fares, just float on and on to wherever I have to go. But to become a cloud, the water has to vaporize. It has to give up its fluidity, its tendencies, its tendency to stick together, its molecules to stick together into what we call water; and if it is condensed into ice it is stuck. Think of the South Pole and the North Pole and the Antarctic and the Arctic ice, which are not melted for millennia, where even dinosaurs have been found embedded in that ice, living probably, I don't know, five hundred million years ago.

So you see, solidity is death. Fluidity is the beginning of life. The ability to float free of all encumbrances means vaporization. So we have to be ready to be vaporized into a state of non-being. Non-being in the sense of non-physical being, where only my love for him is in my heart, and that heart is invisible, yet it is there. That is what we carry through life, through another life, and through yet another life, and which we have carried for I don't know how many lives so far. Part of it is samskara. When the samskara is removed, there comes the original heart in its original pristine divinity and beauty and glory, and being of that nature, which is similar to the Master's, union is possible.

No two things which are different can unite. Water and oil do not mix. A cow cannot mate with a dog. All these are well known genetic facts, breeding facts. Interspecies mating is impossible. So to mate with the Ultimate, to have that ultimate union which we call yoga, to have it as a possibility — He being nothing, cannot change. I being something, must change to become that nothing, so that this nothing and that nothing becomes one nothing. So that is our goal, that is our aim, that is the beauty of Sahaj Marg. I recommend it to all of you for your attention. Thank you.

Nothingness

April 11, 1993, Evening

I thought I had finished what I had to say this morning, but you know, what I really came to say I had left out. We know from Babuji's teachings, from Lalaji's teachings, that God has no mind. We know from our experience that God has no heart. I learned also from Babuji Maharaj that God has limitations, and this was not a joke, it was a very serious statement. He said "God has limitations," and he said, "The most important one is, he can never produce one like himself," whereas a Master of calibre can go on producing a *parampara*, as we call it, you know, a hierarchy of gurus, one after the other, all like himself. So this is a severe and a very serious limitation that we face when we think of God in the context of worship through religion. There is no possible hope in religion, through religious practice, that our prayers will be answered because there is nobody to hear; that our sufferings will be mitigated, because there is nobody to feel what we are suffering; or that we will become like Him, because His single limitation is He cannot make anybody like Himself. Therefore, Babuji often said, "What can God do for you?" To me, when I first heard this, I thought my Master was an exceptionally arrogant man! He mitigated, or shall we say, diluted that arrogance — seeming arrogance, apparent arrogance — by saying, "Whereas Lalaji could do anything." And I said, "What is the proof that Lalaji could do?" He said, "Sit in meditation. We can show you what is possible."

I remember once, my father was wanting to go to Badrinarayan. You know we are Vaishnavaites by birth, and it is a sort of a Mecca for the Brahmin *vaishnav* — Badrinath. We went to Shahjahanpur to participate in a wedding, and after that we were supposed to go to Badrinath. My father went to get his permission. He said, "What you are looking forward to in Badrinath I will give you right here. Sit in meditation." And he did give it. I mean, the instances are too numerous to either mention or to catalogue or to specify. We have all seen — the serious ones, the sincere ones — we have seen the manifestation of his divinity, which we have never seen in a place of worship in any religion. We have seen beautiful idols, we have seen ugly idols. We have seen jeweled idols, we have seen unadorned idols. We have seen poor pundits, we have seen rich pundits. That is all the difference — physical differences from temple to temple, but nowhere, let me assure you — I have been an ardent temple-goer before I came to Babuji Maharaj, I did *veda-parayan* myself. I learned it from a pandit for several years. I was a *vaishnav* Brahmin wearing the *dhoti* in the typical traditional *vaishnav* fashion — bare body, *tilak* on my forehead, and a minimum of three hours of Vedic chant per day, which I can do even today because you don't easily forget these things! And my Master said, "What did all this give you?" I said, "A love of the Vedic chant." "Yes," he said, "You can get it by listening to records!" And the funny thing is, all over India you will find today people are playing gramophone records early in the morning and pretending they are worshipping the Lord.

Throughout the four southern states you will find the *suprabhatam* of Venkatachalapati, you know — Lord Venkateshvara of the Tirupati hills. Five-thirty in the morning you can start hearing this chant, "*Kausalya supraja rama purva...,*" it goes on for about one hour. The man is shaving, the wife is preparing the coffee, the children are doing their homework, and this is going on as some sort of background chanting, and the neighbours are very happy, "Look what a pious neighbour we have!" The day starts with *divyanama* —

Nothingness

the recitation of the Lord's name. Where has it got us? As Babuji has written in *Reality at Dawn*, "All this clamour and noise is spoiling the heaven, the peace of heaven." These are his words if I remember right. All the bell tolling, all the loud chanting, all the wailing, all the rolling around in the mud at his feet.

I have often said that if God were really aware of what is going on, He would be nauseated with His creation. His priests cheating Him, his devotees belying Him, denying Him, most of humanity even going to the extent of saying there is no God. And of course, the major religions all quarreling over "Where is God?", "Who is God?", and "My God is bigger than your God," while all the time saying that there can be only one God, there cannot be a second God. Therefore even in Lenasia we have temples, we have mosques, we have churches, we have Swami Narayan, we have so many things, you see, all clashing, everybody wanting to make the most noise. Then the one who makes the most noise is shut down by the other who is number two in noise-making, so that he can be number one in noise-making. And the powers that govern us are only interested in keeping peace, so they say, "Please, turn down your loudspeakers. I don't deny your right, but please, in the interest of communal harmony, reduce your volume a bit."

So when these limitations are there, in worship of God through traditional religion, any religion, it is amazing that, if anything, it is growing and growing and growing, that even in the remote parts of this world priests are being imported to do what essentially we should be doing ourselves. I have considered the Hindu religion probably the most corrupt of all religions. You'll excuse me for saying this, because this idea that I can hand over my spiritual responsibility to somebody else to perform, calling him the *yajaman*, and that he does, and I will benefit, is a travesty of the truth — it is a lie. Only he who does will get, and if anybody is to get anything it should be the priest, not the *yajaman* who has hired the priest's services. And because the priest's services are hired, he skips most of the mantras. If any of you had ever learned any of these mantras you would know that priest doesn't repeat even ten percent of what he should repeat. And he gets away with it. He gets his silks, he gets his Datsun, and later on a BMW, and he is happy! Where are we, the worshippers? We are where we always were because we are not worshipping, we are handing over — you know, giving him what in legal parlance we would say is a power of attorney. In between God and his devotee there can be no *dalal*, said Babuji Maharaj, and the priest is a *dalal*. At least you Gujarati *dalals*, you do something — you go to a client, you go to a supplier, you bring the two together and you take your commission. These fellows in temples — we go to them, but do they have an access to the other party to the transaction? How can they fulfil their *dalali* if they have no access to the God to whom we would expect them to approach on our behalf?

So you see, the whole thing is a myth, it's a fallacy, it's a crime. Babuji said this in very explicit terms in *Reality at Dawn*. He said gods are only functionaries of nature. Like I am working for my Master, not for you, they work for their Master, who is the ultimate God, not for us. Therefore they don't do anything for us. They cannot, they are not empowered to do it.

The word *permitted* is very important in this context, when it is used in relation to preceptors. There is no question of qualification in Sahaj Marg. I know some people today

Nothingness

claim that they are under the direct instructions of Babuji Maharaj, and they can do this, that, and the other, and that they are qualified or able to do it. I must correct this impression in your minds, of those who are here, because here it needs permission. I often use a slightly vulgar example, you see, that any man can produce a child out of any woman, but if they are not married there is no permission to do it. There is no legal permission, there is no moral permission, there is no spiritual permission. That a man can indulge in an act does not give him the right to do it — or a woman, for that matter. I can also set fire to a house. What does it take? I can destroy a whole complex. How long does it take? A single bomb planted in a nice position.

You know, I have often thought, when this world has to be destroyed, this universe has to be destroyed — all that the Master will do is to quietly place a very subtle transmission at the particular point which you call the Centre, because even the tiniest explosion there will radiate out in all directions and scatter this universe into bits and pieces. It doesn't need any high technology. It doesn't need explosives. It only needs the permission of the Almighty, and a little ability to transmit. You know, sound waves can destroy — the walls of Jericho, and the trumpet. Sonars, lasers, they can destroy. So what does it need to destroy? Nothing.

What does it need to create in us a new human being, a new person, one who from his animal level of existence is going to the divine level of existence? That needs capacity, that needs courage, that needs conviction, that needs patience. It needs more and more than anything else — love from the mind. God — no mind, no heart — cannot love human beings, and cannot love anything else. He is love, but he cannot love. We, on the other end of the spectrum — we can love, but we are not love. Therefore comes this, you know, blindingly illuminating concept that we have not to love, but to become love. We are all — at least we think we are all — capable of loving. Some of us have loved profusely, if I may say so. We have loved cattle, we have loved cats, dogs, many women, many children, many jobs, many things in life, but the experience of loving the many does not seem to give us the capacity to love even the one.

Therefore Babuji says, "Love." And how to create this? Love the Master. Love Him who loves all. He is the only person who can ever have the capacity to love all. We cannot even love our brothers. We cannot love our neighbours. How many of you are at peace with your neighbours, or with your own brothers in your home, or with your *bhabis* and your *behnois*? How many of you are at peace with them and harmony with him? Where is the family which has not partitioned its assets? Success is followed by partition. Failure brings unity in the family. One famous mystic of England — I don't remember a second example — he has given a beautiful example. In winter when it is snowbound, when the country is freezing, everything dying, you put a few crumbs of bread on the window sill, and all the sparrows will come and eat it co-operatively, each giving place to the other. In the fullness of spring when nature is bountiful, you throw a whole loaf of bread outside the window, one sparrow will sit on it and keep everybody else away.

Prosperity is bad. We need enough. We don't have to be prosperous. So when we pray to Babuji Maharaj for prosperity, he smiles a compassionate smile. You know, compassion is necessary not for the criminal, so much. It is necessary for the stupid — for the educated stupid, for the intelligent stupid, who know that one hundred rands is enough but they

Nothingness

want one hundred million. And Babuji is compassionate. He says, "Yes, in your foolishness you have lost all sense of what you need. Now you are in the universe of wants, and wants have no end." Therefore he said, "You have a right to expect your needs to be fulfilled, but not your wants." Wants are many. Needs are few. As a distinct and direct, shall we say, corollary to this he said, "Simplify your existence. Be simple and in tune with nature."

When one lives a simple life one has few needs. One who has few needs, needs not much money — that is easily acquired, morally acquired, acquired with a certain dignity which goes with rightful earning, a fearlessness which goes with rightful earning — one need not be afraid of the police, the income tax man, or even of one's own conscience. Then we find this miraculous feature that now there is enough or more time than we need to meditate, to do our cleaning, to practise constant remembrance, all this blah, blah, blah of spirituality, which we say now we have no time for, because Bachubhai goes to a shop at seven, comes back at eleven at night. Somabhai goes at six-thirty and comes back at eleven-thirty. Amritbhai is never at home. He is traveling all over the world to get business. How can we meditate? And then they start asking very funny questions. If I were to tell the truth about such questions, I don't know what I should do. They come and ask me, "Am I not responsible for my family?" A man who doesn't see his wife once in a year, who does not know in which class his children are studying, often doesn't even know their names — he claims to be in a position of responsibility to his family, and therefore he has no time to meditate. And he points his finger at me and says, "You are wandering around like an *anari*, neglecting your family! Your wife is sick. Your son is working for you. You are feeding off his earnings, and your grandchildren are desolate without you. Are you not neglecting your work, Chariji? Are you not neglecting your responsibilities?"

You know, they are very adroit, some of these intelligent fools — rich fools — at apparently turning the blade upon the one who is wielding the sword. Don't fool yourself by asking such stupid questions. He knows his work. Do you know your work? He knows his responsibilities because he is committed to them. Have you any sense of commitment except to yourself? Do you love your wife, except for her beauty and for the silks that she is wearing? When she dies, God forbid, are you worshipping and praying for her, or are you thinking of yourself and saying, "Oh God, what will I do now? Who will look after me? Who will wash my clothes?" Which husband has mourned his wife? He is only thinking of sex — "*Ayo!* She is gone. What can I do now?" It's a very convenient way, you see, of fulfilling one's responsibilities because, poor fellow, he is so desolate, he doesn't have a wife to fulfil his responsibilities upon, so he takes a second wife — how simple, how easy, and how satisfying to the husband. This right we deny to our women in India. They cannot immediately get hold of a man and marry. "*Pativrata shiromani.*" They are condemned to widowhood. They must not look at a marriage because they will cast evil eyes upon it. They should feed last. They should wash the *bartans*, no? When the husband in a family dies, that woman becomes the servant of the family, in India.

So all women should think, you know, what their husbands are doing when they are supposed to be going around earning money left and right for **their** sake. It is a lie. They are cheating themselves. They are cheating their families. They are cheating God. They are working for themselves. No less a person than Yagnavalkya, the great *rishi,* said this in

Nothingness

the Brihadaranyaka Upanishad to his wife. When his wife wanted spiritual instruction he started by telling her, "Not for the sake of the wife is the wife dear to the husband, my dear. She is dear to the husband for his sake. Not for the sake of the children are the children dear to the father, my dear. They are dear to the father for the sake of the father."

"My children — my son comes first, my daughter has married a millionaire, she has six Mercedes Benz cars in her garage, a house worth six million rand, and we are proud of our daughters." We are not loving our daughters, we are not loving our sons. We are either proud or unproud of them. And when they don't succeed so well in life — our pride is hurt, our ego is hurt and we say, "*Ullu ka pattha*. How can I show my face in society? Will they not say this is Bachubhai's son? You have brought *badnami* on the family." What *badnami*? Poor fellow, he did his best. Today, a man who sells potatoes or bananas and becomes a millionaire is thought more highly of in society than a man who is a professor of philosophy in the university.

Excuse me, but I have to tell you some unsavoury truths. Babuji said all this. He also told me in Paris in 1982 at that tragic moment when he renounced his life, I am sure, he said, "I have been a failure in my life, because I never told the truth to people. I said yes to everything. *Har ek ke haan me haan hum milate gaye. Hum murabat mein aa gaye, logonke. To yeh stithi par pahunche ke aaj hame shak hai ke kaise Lalaji ko apne chehere dikhacon.*" I am exactly quoting what he told me in 1982 August, probably thirty-six hours before we went back home, and from which he never recovered. He was in misery, that man. And why? Because of so-called devotees flocking to him, here as everywhere else, priding themselves upon their devotion, priding themselves for their so-called love for the Master, priding themselves on the fact they gave him one meal, or stitched a coat for him or bought a pair of shoes for him, but not doing what he wanted them to do, not becoming what he wanted them to become. My Master was betrayed by his devotees, by his *bhaktas*, by his lovers more than by anybody else.

Let us not repeat this tragedy again, because now we are betraying ourselves. Having betrayed him, he is no more left for us to betray again and again. Fortunately for him, he has gone to his Master. He told me that he will surely live till 2006, maybe 2007. I mean, he had no business to die in 1983. Twenty-five years before his own time, as stated by him, and I don't think he was reflecting the opinion of astrologers. It was his own predetermined destiny that he would live till 2007. I think he gave up out of utter despair, utter misery, and said, "Now **you** try your best. What can you do? Let us see." Of course, I must agree that what my Master could not do I will probably not be able to do. At the same time, I cannot but say that what my Master hoped for me I have to fulfil — it is my duty. And if in that fulfilment of my duty it becomes necessary to take the stick — as I said yesterday, you must give the right to one you call your Master to beat you if necessary, beat sense into your head, into your bodies, into your stomachs. Only if you give that permission to him, who is unfortunately bound in the situation, can he hope to redeem his vows to his own Master.

Now many people ask me one question. They ask, "Why, if your Master is all powerful, even beyond what God can do, can he not transform us without our co-operation?" I am asked this question repeatedly. "Why should I meditate? What is meditation, after all? Why can't you excuse us this meditation? You know, we want to be transformed — it is

Nothingness

not as if we don't want to be transformed. But you know, responsibilities to family, business partners — what should we do? Why don't you just tell your Master to compulsorily do it for us?" I said, "If that was possible, this universe need not have lasted so long! It would have been created, perfected and destroyed in that one instance of time. He would have created the universe, perfected it in a single instant, or less, and the work is finished. The universe need not exist, He need not exist — they shake hands and part.

The whole problem of spirituality is like the problem of a marriage — willing submission to the partner. Otherwise, we will have in spirituality what is called 'rape', where there is no permission in the relationship between the sexes. Spiritual rape, like physical rape, is not permitted, is immoral, is unjustified. It is not permitted. Therefore, the need to submit. Therefore, the need to open our hearts. Therefore, the need to say, "My Lord, my heart is open. Walk in." Then he smiles gently and says, "This was what I expected of you. *Aapse yahi ummeed thi.*" This was something he repeated again and again. "*Aapse yahi ummeed thi.*" For him it was nothing new because that was what he was wanting all along, there was no song and dance. There was no need to go around yelling at the success, "Eureka, I have got it!" Just a gentle sigh of relief that at least one person has opened his heart to him!

So, spiritually speaking, I would suggest that as God has one limitation — that He cannot make one like Himself because He doesn't have the capacity or the power necessary — God does not have these — in spirituality the Master has a limitation, too: that until you permit, he can do nothing for you. But everybody says, "I have got something, my business has grown, my partner is behaving better with me, my wife is more even-tempered, my children are doing better in school."

Heart of the Lion

Yes. As Babuji has himself written in *Voice Real*, "When people come to me, I consider it a matter of etiquette to give them the minimum benefit that I can afford them, which is material benefit." This they get, and they are happy. They say, "Oh, I have got so much. What more is left?" What about spirituality? "No, no! All this Babuji has given. This house Babuji built for me. This car, with Babuji's grace I bought. My son who was failing for seventeen years has now succeeded. My partners who were robbing me left and right are now back on the green side of the ledger. *Babuji yeh bhi kar dalenge*, you know. After all, for him spirituality is the easiest thing. Why should he not do that for us when he has given me my house, my car, my beautiful wife, my recalcitrant children transformed, my lying and cheating partner transformed. Why should he not do that, Chariji? After all, for him spirituality, as he himself says, 'With a blink of the eye, the Master can give you liberation!'"

So you see how we cheat ourselves? When we get something, how we cheat ourselves? When we don't get something...! So what can that poor fellow do? Does he stop giving? No, because it is his nature to give. As I said, the sun does not stop shining because the housewife has not put out the wet clothes to dry. He doesn't wait to rise, and says, "No, no, Maltiben has not put out the clothes yet. Let me delay rising today by six minutes, or half an hour." He comes and goes, does his job. Are we benefiting by his presence in the fullest possible manner, in the spiritual manner for which alone he has come? For this, have we understood that we have to open our hearts by ourselves? Are we able to submit to him and say, "Here I am, do with me what you will. Make of me what you think is right. Kill me, bury me, re-create me — I don't care. Who am I to say when and where and how this miracle of transformation should happen? You are the

Nothingness

Master. You know what to do, when to do it, how to do it, and why to do it. I am yours. Take me."

Until we have taken this step, I am afraid spirituality will be confined to such petty material benefits as we can get from him, because of his eternal and divine love for humanity which he gives to all. It is a fallacy to think that only abhyasis get. Everybody gets. For him, his dog was granted liberation, and it is a sorrow for me, you see, that his dog was liberated — a calf was liberated during one Basant when it was dying, and he who was eating his lunch suddenly got up, washed his hands with his meal unfinished, and said, "Parthasarathi, *chalo* (come)." We went to the hedge at the back, and there this calf was dying. Nobody thought of it. It saw him and said, "Moo," and expired.

It is a great tragedy, you see, that his cow was transformed, his dog was transformed, but we human beings are not transformed because we are resisting transformation. We are the people for whom he came. We are the chosen ones for whom he gave his life. Yet, his dog benefits, his cow benefits — we are still where we are, because we are conceited, we are happy, we are pleased with ourselves, with what we see in the mirror, with what we see in our passbooks for the bank, and with the gloating admiration and envy that we see in those who look at us. All indications of nothing more than a superficial material advancement in our life which is not going to last. When we die we leave everything behind. Babuji Maharaj said again and again, "Make sure that you have that wealth alone which you can carry with you when you leave this life." And that wealth is not of this world. Thank you.

Pain

April 13, 1993

Yesterday evening we had some talks. Luz Sigl spoke about pain, character formation, and other things — of mice and men. There is one article written by Babuji Maharaj. It has been published in the Patrika, it is part of *Voice Real*, and it is strange but many people don't read it. It is called My Pain. There, Babuji Maharaj writes about his own pain, you see, and in his inimitable concern for us, love for us, in his inimitable etiquette, he claims that pain to be only for himself. He says, "But it is for me alone," and he also told me once or twice that Lalaji Maharaj had assured him that others would not have to suffer that pain. When I first heard this I was shocked. I was annoyed, too, shall we say, because how could I imagine my Master having something in which I could not share? I would not be a true son if I wanted only the golden apples and a share in his house — I mean spiritual house, of course — and eventually, when he nominated me as his successor, it would have been a living lie to refuse to share, except in his totality.

So pain became probably the most important inheritance that I have received from my beloved Master. I welcomed it and I was grateful to him, because on one occasion in Shahjahanpur at midnight we were discussing so many things, including whether there are ghosts; what is a *brahmarakshasa*; and how to deal with them if one should meet them, and he very affectionately and smilingly offered to call a *brahmarakshasa* for me to see. Now ghosts are one thing of which I am very afraid, you see, so I told him, "No, Babuji, I don't want to see a ghost — not even a *brahmarakshasa*." He said, "Why are you afraid? If you should meet one, just say you are Ram Chandra's disciple and it will run away." I said, "Babuji, please spare me this one experience, because I am not happy with ghosts." He laughed and he said "All right, but remember that sometimes in the future, when you are given the work that I am now doing, you may have to deal with ghosts, *brahmarakshasas*, too." I said, "Lalaji has spared you so much. Why don't you spare me some of this?" Then he told me Lalaji never spared him. One of the first assurances Lalaji gave him, or a promise he made to him, was that he shall not have a single moment of rest. Babuji said, "*Hujoor*. I accept." The second was that for any breach in his work, though nobody else would ever be punished, he would be punished. Babuji Maharaj said, "*Hujoor*. I accept." And then of course the third thing was, "You have become me and I have become you, and now none can any more say that there is any difference between you and me." Babuji Maharaj said he wept, and said, "How can I ever be like you?", and Lalaji, in the spiritual sense, embraced him and said, "You already are, because you are my son."

Then Babuji smiled very lovingly at me and said, "You want to become like me, isn't it?" I said, "Yes." He said, "Then everything I have suffered, you have to suffer." So you see, it was at the same time a promise, a gift, and a sentence. Now I considered myself extraordinarily blessed that he gave me three gifts all in one — a blessing, a gift, and a sentence. And he did add that he would always be with us, guiding my work from above — and you know, because I was tending to be a little upset with all this, what I thought, morbid talk about when he goes away, what I will become, and all that, I said, "Babuji, I don't want to hear of your passing." He said,

Pain

"Don't worry, I'll be here for a long time — till 2006, 2007," and then he gave me a short talk on the value of pain. He said, "Fools run away from pain. Those who wish to become saints have always embraced pain and have asked for more and more." Sometimes to the extent that, according to Babuji Maharaj, even God is surprised. He said, "How can I give you **more** pain?"

Now, whenever I speak of pain and death in the West, in the Occidental countries, there is always a little fear in the abhyasis, a little resentment perhaps — quite a bit of anger. "Why is this blighter talking to us about these unsavoury matters? Did not Babuji Maharaj say, 'It is for me alone.' Why is he talking of this pain?" Even to speak about pain is not welcomed by people. They think that it is a threat. They would accept any other gift — gifts of love should not confer pain! Isn't it? But every woman knows that the first gift of love that she receives is an enormous dose of pain when she has her first baby. No child is born without pain to the mother. Physical pain? Yes, it is easy to bear with. What about the subsequent pain of bringing up that child? All the worries that we suffer from. Every time the child goes to school, the mother has a trauma, you see, especially in countries like the United States where every mother is afraid whether the child will come back, whether somebody will, you know, kidnap it, rape it. Who knows what can happen between going to school and coming back from school? Then we realise that pain is a part of life. Pain is very much a part of life. I would go a step further and say, "Life is pain."

Psychologists — there are some here — may give other definitions. But human beings we all are. Any one of you have just but to look into yourselves to find that inside you there is nothing but pain, which is perhaps one reason why we are so anxious to have some pleasure in life, why we are frantically looking for pleasure, for fun: to try, and in some way remove this pain which is inside. But the wise man, if he is wise, the wise woman, if she is wise, soon understands that this pain is not of this world. It is a pain born with us. It is a pain created by the soul's longing to return to its source, to its original home, as Babuji Maharaj said, and until we do that, this pain cannot go. So any frantic search for pleasure in which to forget this pain, deaden this pain, dull this pain, is as good as taking narcotics — drugging ourselves insensate.

So you see, pleasure is our enemy. It makes us forget our pain, even if it is only a momentary forgetfulness, and in that moment of forgetfulness of this pain, we only remember the pleasure, and we want to heighten it, embroider it, make it bigger and bigger. Ultimately, if it is pursued in that single-minded pursuit, it can go to the extent of suicide. The only way of removing this pain is by taking a positive step and going towards the source to which this pain indicates, and try to find our way back home. Like a weary traveler going back home, when he can say, "Aha, I am back home. Now everything is forgotten. No more pain, no more frustration, no more dust of the journey, no more heat, no more uncertainties." So you see, the only way of easing our pain, of removing our pain, is not by psychological methods, not by clinical methods, not by medical means, not by going to, you know, casinos, getting drunk, not in women, not in drugs, not in possessions, not in gold, not in silver, but in wisely turning away from this life — outward life, physical life, sensual life — to a truly spiritual inner search for the origin of that pain.

Pain is the beacon of a lamp lit in the windows of our original home, shining out in the darkness, and we have only to follow it back. We are the ancient mariner to whom that

Pain

lamp beckons. It is a lighthouse guiding us back. Pleasure diverts. Pleasure makes us deviate from our path. Pleasure pulls us down into ignominy, into insult, into bestiality, until we lose all semblance of a human existence. Our wisdom is lost, our wealth is lost, our health is lost, our bearings are lost, and in that state of friendship and pleasure we have only friends similarly positioned in life — they can only drag us down into that mire, into that cesspool, into that whirlpool of misery and sickness and loss. Like unfortunate friends who do not know how to swim, trying to help a drowning man — all drown together. Pleasure is where people drown together. Pain is where one can find his way back home alone, being guided by pain in the right direction, provided we accept it. Provided we accept that pain is the fortunate, the divine remnant in me, created by my longing for my original home. Longing for not only going home, but to be united with my Beloved who is waiting for me there, and then it becomes an unerring guide and beacon to guide me back. So you see, we should know the real value of pain. Otherwise we will tend, like the Occidental people, to avoid pain.

Babuji always said that he was afraid of India developing materially. He said, "This land is not destined for material growth, for material welfare, because if it happens it would be a tragedy. Spirituality would be destroyed." Perhaps that is why India remains — materially, outwardly — a poverty-stricken country, and therefore people in millions turn towards this destiny of theirs, in however, you know, unsuccessful a way it may be, but the trial is there. The effort is there, and no effort, no trial, goes unrewarded. Therefore, India has always been, and will always be, the true spiritual guiding force in this world. A spiritual force which releases the pain in us, makes of individual pain a cosmic pain, a divine pain, and, shall I say, converts it into something which is for our evolution, for our guidance back to our source which can never fail, which is infallible.

One who follows pleasure, follows only dreams, chimeras. Pleasure doesn't really exist. That which exists eternally is the true existence. Therefore, pain which follows us from life to life, through life after life, until we have the wisdom to go back to our original home, is an eternal facet of our existence. I would say it is the sub-stratum of human existence. That being so, can we remove this pain by taking our own life in an act of criminal suicide? Not at all. We are only adding to the pain. One more level of pain attached to the already existing pain, because of our disgust with ourselves, of our inability to look at ourselves even in a mirror, perhaps, and in a gesture of ultimate denial of the self, one gives up his self. But the Self inside cannot be given up. The purpose of our existence has not been fulfilled.

Please remember that rebirth is not a punishment given by God. In rebirth each one has an opportunity for a fresh life, to again start this journey, find one's way and reach one's goal. It is a fresh opportunity that nature gives us again and again and again and again. Rebirth is not a punishment. It is like a schoolboy who is retained in one class because he has not passed the examinations of that class. It is not a punishment by the school. It is his inability to cope with the needs of that class, which says, "Brother, if you cannot cope with the needs of this class, how are you going to cope with the needs of the next higher class? How can you cope with a higher responsibility when you are unfit for the lower responsibilities?"

So you see, nature gives us, I think without limit, eternally — chance after chance after chance, which we call rebirth and death, and not understanding, in our foolishness,

Pain

in our fear of death, that this is like a new day, a new page in a book, to write upon, you see, and create for ourselves a new future. I am surprised that people are afraid of death when it is life they should be afraid of. What is there to be afraid of in death? Every fool dies. Every millionaire dies. Every king has died. *Avatars* have died. Who has not died? That which is the common and only heritage of all human beings — can it be fearful? Can it be something of which we should be afraid? Is it not only a door into the next life which beckons and says, "Forget this room full of horrors. Come into this room, where it is all beatitude, plenitude, love."

So you see, it is **life** we should be afraid of. Babuji Maharaj told me — I think it was in 1972 or '73 when he said, "I have given you everything." I am not talking of powers, because powers are irrelevant in Sahaj Marg — but of condition, you see. It was in '76, perhaps, I'm not sure. We were sitting in the Copenhagen airport waiting for a flight, he and I opposite each other, when he said, "Is there time before the flight?" I said, "Yes, they should be announcing it shortly." He said, "Sit in meditation." And just as I closed my eyes and adjusted myself and started to meditate, he said, "That's all." It lasted forty seconds. It was a famous sitting which everybody in the Mission knows about, because when he went home he told Satya Pal — some of you may have heard of him — "I have given Parthasarathi a sitting such as I have not given to anybody, nor will I ever give it to anybody." So Satya Pal asked him, "Why to Parthasarathi alone?" He said, "Because of his love and devotion. You know, he has traveled with me for three months, and not once did he think of his home or his family! He was totally lost in me." Then Satya Pal said, "Okay, what did you give him?" He said, "To others I give something. To him I transmitted my **own** condition."

So you see, the rewards of pain are tremendous. The awards of remembrance — what do you get when you remember the beloved? You get the beloved. You don't ask for him to come in a Cadillac, dressed in a velvet suit, and toting a sidearm. Love's reward is the beloved. I mean, this is a lesson for every girl and for every boy. When they also start asking, "How much does she bring with her? Does she have a house? Will she have a big dowry? Does she have a car?", we are demeaning love. It is not just merely *sauda*, as we say in India, you see — marketplace trading. It is a demeaning of love, and love cannot be demeaned. All morality is not an infringement upon the individual's liberties and rights. It is a protection of this sacredness, this divinity of love. "Thou shalt not sully love." Love cannot be sullied. Love cannot be tainted. Love cannot be bought and sold. But unfortunately we believe, you see, that our liberties are being restricted, we are being restrained, this order is stupid. As John Barlow said about seating separately — there was a huge uproar! He put it very mildly. It lasted a couple of years! But, tenacity, you see — the tenacity of love! Which is what a mother has for her child. She will not give up easily where her child is concerned. The father will say, "Throw this damned thing out!" Mother — no. She has produced it, she has borne the pain, she has suffered. She knows what she has undergone. Deformed baby? She will say, "Yes. My baby. You get the hell out of here!"

So you see, that is love. That is why in India, the love of the mother is so praised, praised beyond all love, beyond even the love of God himself. *Mamta*, it is called. Maternal love. And now, if a mother is going to be merely, you know, an instrument of pleasure — handed from hand to hand, sold perhaps — where is that love? Where is that sacredness of love? Where is that divinity behind that love? Therefore, you

Pain

see, marriage is not just a piece of paper as some of our Western abhyasis used to tell me. "But Chari, it's only a piece of paper." I said, "Why are you afraid of that piece of paper, then? If it's just a piece of paper, just a formality — sign it!"

Love must bring commitment. A mother's commitment to her child must be total, not just for a beautiful baby, you see, which looks very angelic, as if it is painted by Rembrandt or somebody like that. Or a Rafael — blue-eyed, cherubic, angelic. To the zebra, a zebra child is an angel. To the lion, a lion cub is an angel. To a human, a human baby is an angel. It is a gift of God. It is a gift of love. And when we say love is God — well, it is a gift of God, too.

So you see, out of pain only is born this inordinate, or, shall I say, enormous capacity for love, because we are able to love that for which we have suffered most. In another talk, I referred a few days back to the love that a mother has for a child who is less endowed than normally endowed. How much she suffers with it, suffers for it, suffers over it. For the happy, healthy child we don't need to suffer. But a special child — you know, I came across only one woman in all my life, who everybody thought was cursed by being given a child which was deformed. She said, "I am blessed." I said, "Yes? You really think so?" She said, "Yes. To me, God has done the signal honour of presenting this child, knowing that I will look after it, love it, cherish it no less than another child. He did not give this child to other women who would have probably cursed God, cursed themselves, prayed for its early death. It is a gift of His infinite love to me."

So you see, pain is a gift from God. "Accept miseries as blessings," Babuji says in one of his maxims. What on earth for? What is suffering? When Babuji went to Fatehgarh to see Lalaji and landed there at nine o'clock at night in dead

Heart of the Lion

winter, the household was dark. Everybody had gone to bed. He slept on a stone step outside Lalaji's house, like a dog curled up there. That is love for the Master. He didn't knock and say, "Hey Master, where's my room?" Here, if we don't have a mattress, people go into agonies. They get a mattress — they go into ecstasies. What is this agony and ecstasy business? Just a mattress between you and your love for Master? Babuji slept a whole night — perhaps the temperature was zero or just below zero — with nothing, not even a shawl around him. Next morning, when Lalaji opened the door and he saw Babuji, he said, "Ram Chandra, you have been sleeping here all night." He said, "No, no, I just came and the house was closed. How could I disturb your honour? *Hujoor ko hum kaise jagate.*"

See, we talk too much of love, petty love. "Oh, I love this boy." "I love this girl." What is this love of which we are speaking? Is there pain behind it? You see, like the paper currency of former times used to be backed by gold. Our love must be backed by pain. If there is no pain in our love, shun it. It is the other four-letter word — lust. You know, I was told love is a four-letter word. Perhaps there is a song like that. Yes. L-O-V-E, or L-U-S-T. When it is L-U-S-T the pain is for the other. When it is L-O-V-E the pain is for you. Therefore, those who are unwilling to face pain, bear pain, welcome pain — of course they will get something. Babuji said, "To everybody who comes to me — etiquette demands I throw him a few crumbs of spirituality." We don't want to be treated like dogs — a crust of bread. We want to be treated as the beloved. When we knock He must open the door. His face must light up with pleasure, with joy, with love, and He must embrace us on the doorstep. That is the reward that pain brings.

Pain

The reward that pleasure brings, as I have already said, is derogation of the self, fall from values, sensual excess, failing health, failing wealth, failing wisdom. So one should not consider it inappropriate if I said, "Pleasure leads to hell, and pain to heaven." All of us should realise that if in this immense human heritage, the only heritage that a human has which is a universal endowment of God — everything else God gives, or seems to give, in bits and pieces to selected people. Some are rich, some are wise, some are healthy, but all are in pain. Therefore pain is the common factor in human existence. It is the only thing that God can have given to us. Air, sunlight, water — and pain! We don't have to pay for these things. They are ours to be used intelligently, to be used wisely as an infallible guide for us to return home. Only then will our pain go, and not pleasure but **bliss** be our portion for the next stage of existence, when we are hand in hand, arm in arm, hugging each other — me and my Beloved.

So I just wanted to put these thoughts before you. Next, I have a very different, you know, a blissful announcement to make. This morning we had a preceptor's meeting, and immediately thereafter I was taken on a sort of a hush-hush mission. I didn't know where I was being taken, but I know the young man who took me there has considerable affection for me and regard. So I said, "Lead on, Jeeves!", and he took me to see a plot of land — 1,200 square meters, approximately 12,000 square feet, located on a street called the Parrot Crescent in Lenasia South, I believe they call it Dakshina, too. And he said, "Do you like this plot?" I said, "Yes, it's a lovely piece of land. Who am I to like or dislike? It's all, you know, good for a meditation hall," and he said, "If you like this land, it is yours for the Mission." They wish to remain anonymous, the donors of this land, but this wish I am not able to respect, because, as I said to that young man, "Smoke and love can never be hidden." It's an old proverb, and this gift of land to the Mission from this family is a gift of their love for the Master. So I have pleasure in saying that our respected brother, Govindbhai Rama and his sons, Chandubhai, Bakulbhai, and Dr. Mukund are the donors of this property. It is their love for the Mission, it is their love for Babuji Maharaj, which has made such a generous gesture possible, which has brought into being the first firm foundation for the Mission's existence in South Africa. It is also a sign of Babuji's immense love for them, that in this materialistic age, they can think of donating a property, which is certainly a valuable property, to the Mission, and may Babuji continue to shower his love upon them. Thank you.

The Purpose of Existence
April 15, 1993

(follows long question by Dr. Mukund: "What is the purpose of my existence?")

Very long question. I have forgotten most of it! I think basically there are two prongs to this answer. One is to know why I am here, and the other is to be what I am here for. Most intellectually inclined people assume that they have to know why they are here before they can be what they are here to be, or to become. My respectful submission is that it is not necessary. Once this is understood, then we have a straight line without a fork, because it is at every fork that this confusion comes. If there is no fork, it's like a straight road, there is no confusion, but if a road forks, you slow down a bit to see which one you have to take. There, the way goes to the destination. Here too, the way goes to the destination. One, in terms of answers, the other in terms of being. So one is intellectual, one is existential. With the intellectual we need not bother. With the existential we are concerned because we are already in existence, so we can't help it. So that is as far as the intellect goes. Do we need an answer? No. Nobody ever needs an answer.

Number two — Dr. Mukund wanted to question every question, question every answer, question every theory. He had to cut things himself to know the truth of what his professors had taught him. Now, that is the way of the child —

excuse me — because the child wants to do everything. Even when the father says, "Don't touch this. It is hot!", it must insist on knowing by touching and then weeping and being kissed by the mother. Father giving it a slap, applying a little ointment on its burnt fingers, and going to work cutting up something else to know for himself, precisely what he forbade the child to know. In a sense, it is this arrogance of thought — that only what I see, I know. But just imagine, you see, the whole of human knowledge, the sum of human knowledge is through transmittal of that knowledge. We are building each generation upon the knowledge of the previous generation. Otherwise we wouldn't have anything — each generation would have to learn what is the difference between the primitives and us. They are not able to transmit knowledge, for paucity of means of expression. They don't have adequate language to speak, to express so many things. They have no means of transmission. And as you all know, it is a philosophical concept as well as a real thing, that until written language was created, until the printing press was invented by Gutenburg, transmission of knowledge was impossible in most of the world except in India. There we had the idea of memorizing whole bodies of texts generation after generation, so that it was transmitted through the memory of man. The Vedas! I mean, imagine that all the Vedas put together, if you recite without omission it would probably take you a whole month to recite it once. You can imagine what enormous feats of memory, what prodigious feats of memory, our forefathers have indulged in, only to transmit it.

So transmission is the essence of existence. Now, they insist upon questioning every little bit of scientific or other knowledge, starting with the amoeba, let us say. It is crazy because we have no time, first of all, to test every piece of knowledge that has been handed down to us. We have, of

The Purpose of Existence

course, to learn what we have to learn, to do what we have to do here in a professional way to earn our living. By the way, it is very petty. It is 'one hair off my head,' as we say. What we really learn, we learn from inherited memories, instincts, and acquired knowledge — three ways of acquiring knowledge. Only yesterday, Mukund himself showed me a film where a zebra stallion is shot down, and that man who made the film was bewailing the fact that with it so much of condensed memory stored in its cells — cellular memories — has gone. Now, a zebra doesn't learn how to hunt or how not to be hunted, how to migrate from this water hole to that water hole six hundred miles away, or six hundred kilometers away, yet it does it. Elephants have been known to traverse distances of thousands of miles, following almost precisely the same routes, generation after generation. It's fascinating to read these things. How? Now, if every elephant wanted to be taught the route — "Go seven miles southwest, hit the first water hole, fill up your belly, avoid the lions." You know, there are these *mahoba* trees or the, whatever it is, you know, they enjoy most. "Then you walk seventy-six miles to the next water hole, then turn east. You have to go through twenty-two miles of desert. Fill up and feel the difference," like the Caltex advertisement! Not at all.

The whole of our existence rests on such acquired knowledge transmitted to us through memory, through cellular structures, through the brain itself. What little we learn, gives us this arrogance that, "I am a learned man. I am an educated man." It is but the tip of the needle. So number one, this has to be understood: that what I learn in this life is like the small bit of stone on the top of an enormous mountain, and on this we rest our pride, our degrees, our education and our sophistication. But if that whole mountain is knocked off from that small pebble resting on top of it, where would the

Heart of the Lion

pebble be? We know this. When a man loses his memory, you know, suffers from lapse of memories — what happens to him? Yet he is still able to live. He has forgotten himself. He doesn't know his name. He has forgotten his marriage. He doesn't know he has two children out in Lenasia. He doesn't know he is a doctor, delivering mothers of their babies. Yet he lives. He knows how to eat, how to defecate, how to walk, how to see, and what he is seeing. From where comes this knowledge? So you see, that is the knowledge on which we exist. The acquired knowledge is that on which we support ourselves: our profession, our work, whether we are teachers or, you know, doctors, or whatever. This is the first point I have to make.

The second point I wish to emphasize is this: all knowledge is gained by experience. It is only the modern intellectual idiot who thinks that he has learned something, and knowledge has to be acquired. When our primitive forefathers lived long ago in the pre-history of the human age, they transmitted knowledge that was knowledge they had experienced in this existence. "Don't touch fire. It burns!" "Water cools. It quenches thirst." This was all experiential knowledge, and I was suggesting to Mukund today, that all our laboratories would be unnecessary except where we are compelled to test hypothetical knowledge for verification. Nobody has built a laboratory to test whether fire really burns, because it's not necessary. Nobody has built a laboratory to test whether water wets, because it's not necessary. But some fellow sits down and, you know, speculates. He lets his mind roam about in the future and says, "If this were so and if this were so, given these two conditions, this could be so," and ergo — we have a laboratory, to test. If the laboratory or experiment proves successful, that hypothetical knowledge becomes fact. If it is not, it goes into the limbo of

The Purpose of Existence

so many untested hypotheses, and tested and failed hypotheses. Therefore it is axiomatic in science that most of scientific knowledge is hypothetical knowledge, to be tested out in the labs, again and again. That is why science is so firmly fixed on repetivity of experiments. Every one of us must be able to repeat an experiment and to prove it for himself. So what are they really doing? It is experiment again. Experiment means — like the French use the word *expérimenter* to denote experience. In the original Latin, there was no such thing as an experiment being an experiment as we understand it today. An experiment meant — an experience.

So the test of knowledge is personal experience. Knowledge acquired through experience, transmitted intellectually, emotionally, mentally, through subsequent generations. Repeatedly tested by us, not by testing it as an objective test, but subjectively through experience of life. A tiger will kill. It is painful. I don't have to go and submit myself to a tiger or a lion in the Serengeti, you know, to feel it! Laceration of the skin produces ulcers. Subsequent infection can kill me. I mean, nobody ever thinks of testing these hypotheses. "Let me be mauled by a lion, Chari! I wish to see for myself how it feels." Well, it's easy to imagine. What we cannot test objectively we can experience in the way of a guided imagination. Not fantasy, but by guided imagination. You know the modern technique of, for instance, a tennis player wanting to perfect his game — he sits in his easy chair, relaxes, and imagines he is playing a game with, say, McEnroe. And it helps his game, but you must have already played a little tennis before this will work!

So you see, we can improve upon anything by mentation, and the perfect mentation is meditation. Meditation means to think constantly about one thing. It is continuous perpetual mentation on one object. Now obviously, most of the things in this universe, or most of the items of knowledge, do not need continuous mentation, therefore need not be meditated upon. What is it, therefore, that we have to meditate upon? That which cannot be known through the sensory apparatus that we have been furnished with — precisely. So should I meditate upon my girlfriend? No, because there are other ways of knowing her — the experiential mode. You want to know what a kiss is like? Kiss and see.

You know, there is the great story of a *rishi* — I am not joking, these are real stories of a *rishi* — who, till the age of sixteen was leading a protected existence in his father's ashram. There were no women, no girls, because the father was afraid the young fellow, very handsome, very tall, very inspiring, very wise, would be spoiled. At the age of sixteen he had to let him go. And he said, "At the border of my ashrams," because he had a vast ashram, "you will come to a river. You have to cross it, and then you are in other lands. May God protect you." He comes to a boat, it is all flower-decked, and damsels are rowing it. He gets into that boat and says, "Take me to this place." Now, the girls are curious. "Who is this handsome fellow?" Very wise, very fair, very handsome, unspoiled, and they want, each one of them, to give him a kiss. But he refuses. He says, "What's a kiss?" Then they say, "It's a fruit. You must taste it." And then he says, "How does it taste?" One girl comes and kisses him on the lips and says, "This is what we call kiss-fruit." Not ice-fruit, kiss-fruit. Like that they entice him into the worldly life. Now this is the story of Rishya Shringa, one of the most famous *rishis* in the Hindu tradition. He had to learn!

We have the story of Adi Shankara, also, who was the perfection of all knowledge. One day he meets a female intel-

The Purpose of Existence

lectual rishi. She scoffs at his knowledge. She says, "Shankaracharya, you? But your knowledge is incomplete." He says, "Nobody has ever dared to tell me that. In what am I incomplete?" She says, "Do you know or have the knowledge of sex? You are a *brahmachari*. What do you know about it?" He puts down his head in shame because he has not had that experience. At that moment, with his *gyanadrishti* — divine vision — he sees that a king has just vacated his body in death. He hangs himself up in the jungle upside down, ties his feet to a branch, and jumps into the body of the king and lives with that queen for six months, learning all about love. One day he feels his fingers being singed, you see, because a hunter has found the body hanging upside down, thought it is a dead body, and is setting fire to it. Immediately he jumps back into his body, because otherwise he would have no body to come back to.

So, whether you will or not, these things have to be learned. No use reading books on sex — even the great Kinsey, you see, or the Kama Sutra. These things have to be learned by experience. It is my submission, again, that nothing is learned but through experience. What you learn through books is only the experience of others who are putting them down in books. Where we need to test it, we test it. Where it is not necessary to test it, we only accept it.

So the inquisitive mind must be to **add** to knowledge, not to **prove** existing knowledge. Inquisitiveness does not mean, test the Einstein theory, test this, test that, test a caesarian. Not at all. To my way of thinking, inquisitive means, going forward into the future with my thought, probing into what else can be. Given the summit on which I am already placed as a mere pebble, how can I make this mountain grow another thousand feet during my existence, so that even though I remain a pebble, the mountain under me has risen by a few thousand feet during my lifetime. We misinterpret 'inquisitive' as applying to past knowledge. "Oh, let me see what this is about." But that has already been tested by generations of human beings. Existential facts such as pain, such as pleasure, such as miseries, such as happiness — these are the heritage, the common heritage, of all human beings. You don't have to speak the language of other human beings to transmit to them pain. What is pain? You pinch a little, and they know. Isn't it?

So inquisitiveness, the need to intellectually probe must be restricted to the future. And again I submit that the best way is meditation. Why? Because only through meditation I can probe into a future which is not yet physical, which is not yet sensory-conditioned, but which can be, if I am able to locate it and bring it into my present. Otherwise we are only dealing with what is already here, about which everything is known, mostly.

I mean, I am amazed when people go into the Amazon or someplace, and discover fifty new varieties of butterfly. So what! You are not discovering anything, you are only naming that which has existed from primordial times. Does naming a thing become an act of discovery? Not at all. Suddenly they find this butterfly — "By jove, I've never seen this," and they catch it in a net and subject it to the torture of being pinned down on a bit of cardboard, and then study it, draw it, patent it — name it *butterflyicus mukundus* in Latin. And he is a discoverer, and he gets a prize, the prize for botany of this year, or for zoology of this year, or if it is sufficiently meritorious in the eyes of other fools who are going to judge his discovery, the Nobel prize for this year. Naming a thing is not discovering the thing. When we discover it, it has no

The Purpose of Existence

name because it is totally new to human existence. Such totally new things in human existence — there are very few of them today. At the same time it can be unimaginably vast.

Now, science says we do not know the ends of this universe. Mukund himself said that. Then how do we suppose there is a universe? We say it is expanding at unimaginable velocities. Have we experienced those velocities? I am on this globe, which is spinning at such a tremendous rate — I do not know the exact speed but it runs into several miles per second — do I experience that? Why do I not experience it? Precisely because I have no point of reference with which to time it. All knowledge is based on a point of reference. When you are moving in a plane which is flying very smoothly, when there are not even clouds, you do not feel your motion because you are part of that which is moving. A child in the womb of its mother does not know it is moving and walking around when the mother is walking around. It is separateness that creates the need for knowledge.

When we fell, or as Babuji put it, when we descended — which has a different meaning altogether from the word 'fell' in Christian theology — this separateness made imperative the need for the knowledge of that which was separate. "Who am I?", first question. And the father is saying, "But you are only a part of me, my son." It did not cut any ice — he said, "Yes, but Dad, who are you?" "I am that I am." This is what you find in the Bible. Not satisfactory — "What the hell do you mean, 'I am that I am'? Tell me more precisely. Are you John?" "No." "Are you Kalalua?" "No." "Are you Mukund?" "No." And then gently smiling like Babuji, he says, "Yet, I am all these, too." "Yes, but Dad, how can you be nothing and everything?" "Find out, my son."

Heart of the Lion

So when we separate ourselves from that existence which we call our original home, like a son who is leaving his father's house and going out in his car, we need maps, we need sandwiches, we need a flask of tea, flashlight for the night, money to spend, credit card for the unknown expenses that we might have to accept. All this becomes necessary because we have left home. For one who is at home, nothing is necessary.

So now what shall I answer further? Therefore, on the way back home — you know, many Europeans come to India for Basant, for Babuji's birthday, and I call myself the wastepaper basket of the Mission, because some leave their sleeping bags, some leave their, you know, unused biscuits — "Chari, give it to somebody." All the medicines that they brought, imagining India to be the land of pestilence and disease, they leave behind. All this I receive, I receive with gratitude, you see, because we should be grateful for what we receive. But it's a funny thing — nobody leaves his money behind! (laughter) And says, "No, no, keep the money! I am going home. I have enough there now." Similarly when we are now going on our way back home, we have to drop things. Why? Because we don't need them anymore. My intelligence? What for? My road maps? What for? I don't need them where I am going. It's precisely for this reason that we say, "Drop these unwanted things. Why are you carrying them on your head? Throw them away, you don't need them anymore."

So there is no such thing as renunciation in Sahaj Marg. This must be very clearly understood, not in the sense of Vishwamitra, you know, who had his fun with Menaka, and then says like this when she brings the child (gestures). A classic gesture of renunciation! (laughter) No! Renunciation

The Purpose of Existence

does not mean license. What we need in this life, legitimately — physical support, emotional support, support of love, what, as Portia puts it, "The law allows it. The court awards it. So let it be."

So we have, for what it is worth, moral sanction for marriage, social sanction for marriage, legal sanction for marriage. But if you go into the higher philosophical sense, is marriage really necessary? I would hesitate to answer no, because it might be misunderstood, but really marriage is a human institution. Why? To prevent the big, strong blighter from taking away the beautiful wife of a weak man who cannot otherwise protect her. So the law steps in to protect. Like property laws — to protect the weak from the grabbing hands of the strong. "This is my plot. Lay off!" "Who says so?" "The law permits it, the court awards it. It is mine."

So as long as we need, or as long as we say, "This is mine, this is mine, this is mine," we need external protection — of law, of society, of custom, of religion. When there is nothing which is mine, I don't need any protection. When I understand that even my life is not mine, but it is His, if at all it needs protection, it needs His protection. It is His property. He will look after it. The plot of land on Parrot Crescent which the family of Mukund has gifted to the Mission did not need protection for itself! It was protected by the owners for themselves. They put up a fence around it. The land did not say, "Protect me." Protect me from what? How can I be protected? I am not a separate piece of land, I am part of this vast globe that you call your earth. **You** have partitioned me into small bits and squares and pieces, you see, and called this agriculture land, this fertile land, that infertile land, that desert. But to me, I am a whole, and whose protection do I need? **You** need protection from me.

Heart of the Lion

I read a story once, you see, which amused me enormously. A man tilling the ground, you know, and telling his friend the farmer, "This is all my land that you see." Hundreds and hundreds of acres and Bhumi is laughing, she says, "This blighter, he is walking on my breast like my child, but the blighter doesn't know he's going to be buried in me soon!" How much land does a man require? Tolstoy — "All of the land we need, and that only for the Christians, too, is the plot of land in which they will be buried — two metres by half a metre, perhaps, or three quarters of a metre by three quarters of a metre — this is all the land that we need." And we are protecting this land? From whom, against whom? Territorial limit — twelve miles — ocean. This is South African sea. Hah! Who gave it to you? There used to be a three mile limit before, and with each successive war, as the ranges of our missiles expand, our coastline is being expanded more and more, the territoriality of that sea is being increased from three miles to twelve miles. It may end up at three hundred miles, I don't know. Then you will have a new war because my neighbor's sea and my sea will be butting against each other, you know, and the three hundred miles here and in between is no-man's sea again.

So when I have nothing, I don't need anybody's protection. If I consider myself as His, He has to protect me. My cows don't need protection. They need protection because they are **my** cows. **I** protect them. The cow is happy to be free. I don't think they like being shut up in a byre, you see, or put in a paddock. They would like to switch up their tails and run around like crazy and roll in the mud. So protection for one is imprisonment for another. You see this in this land. Today, what is going on here, you know — the white man saying, "I want to protect you and educate you until you are able to rule yourself." But then these Matabeles and Zulus,

The Purpose of Existence

they have no sense to ask, "Yes, but white man, before you came we were governing ourselves very well. We were very happy. There was a structure, there was a hierarchy which was rigid, which was respected — which **worked**!" They are not able to say it because the poor people are still in primitive conditions, they have no education, they have no political education, they don't know how to answer these questions, so they suffer, and they react in the only way they know — violence.

So you see, freedom must be given before freedom can be perfected. You cannot tie up a child and say, "I will let you free when you are perfect." How will it become perfect? It must be allowed its liberties. And what should we do? We keep a protective eye upon it. Not restrain it, but watch it! This is what a sensible parent should do. "No, no, you should not go out. Come back before dark!" What is so wonderful about the sun, that it's a protective thing? Don't accidents happen in the daytime? Are not women raped in the daytime? Don't people die in the daytime? Are babies not born in the daytime? What does not happen in the day which happens only at night? Nothing. So why these restrictive things? "Before sunset you must be in." "You shall not go into deep water." Well, for a man who doesn't know how to swim, three feet of water is enough to drown in! He doesn't need deep water. I can drown in sixteen inches! Isn't it? People have been known to drown in their bathtubs!

So it's all crazy. These are limits of ignorance we set to our knowledge. "I climbed a tree. I fell down. Therefore you should not climb a tree." Who said so? You are a fool — you didn't know how to climb the tree properly! "Let me show you," says the arrogant son. And he climbs, he is happy, he throws down a few apples for his old father. He has no teeth, says, "My son, what will I do with these apples?" He says, "Okay, Dad, leave it to me! I know what to do now." Now that is knowledge, you see. My experience again — that which you could not do, old man, in your youth, I am doing in my youth. So don't restrict my, shall we say, impulses towards learning more about myself through myself. Real knowledge is by using myself, through myself, to find my Self. Not myself — my **Self**.

So I repeat — all knowledge was born out of experience. Subsequently it was transmitted through books, through words and what have you. We should not make the mistake of assuming that only what is in books, and what is recited, is knowledge, and therefore I have to write more books. Or think I cannot believe that — therefore I must experiment myself. Not at all. Experiments are conducted only to prove or disprove. Hypothetical foundations of knowledge, which, if they are found untrue, are thrown away. If they are found true, they are further experimented upon to try to repeat them so many times that there can be no doubt about that piece of knowledge.

It is an axiom in science that almost every thirty years, old theories are not only refuted but turned upside down. Only this morning I read in the newspaper that the dinosaurs were perhaps descended from birds! What happens to the pterodactyl, for heaven's sake! And that huge dinosaur, you know, the brontosaurus. It came from a bird? Logic says, "Stupid." Like homoeopathy — you know, allopaths laugh at homoeopathy — "These few globules of medicine, Chari, are going to cure you?" But they believe in big sixteen ounce bottles, you see, and syringes.

Big things have always come from small things. The biggest giant was conceived in his mother's uterus as nothing

The Purpose of Existence

more than a unicellular organism. Then it proliferated. It grew. It assumed the shape of that which it is going to be, already in the womb. It's a well known fact that around three months, three and a half months only, the fetus becomes something perceptibly human. It is well known that this fetus passes through everything that it has evolved through in the past — a shape of a fish, a shape of a lobster — everything is replicated there, but in just three months. Then it becomes perceptibly human. Its limbs start sprouting, and stupid mothers go and want to determine the sex by ultrasound technology.

My daughter-in-law went for such a test and she came back very excited, and very un-girl like, and she said, "Papa, I saw it!" It was a boy, you see. I said, "Shameless one, you are talking of this?" She said, "No, no, but I saw it there!" I said, "Surely you have seen it before!" Now, you see, look at this, you know, funny thing — a married girl who has seen it, felt it, experienced it, yet wants to see it on an ultrasound monitor and satisfy herself, "Yes, it does exist!" This is the modern curiosity — to know what I already know, in a different way. But the real curiosity, I repeat, must be oriented towards the future, towards discovery.

For the French, and in the Latin it is *decouvrir*, to uncover. It's a beautiful word. There is no such thing as discovery. We uncover which is there, which we have never known till now. It is like a wife, you know, removing the lid of a dish and we look inside and say, "Mama mia!" and sit down to eat. I don't discover food, I uncover food. The Veda says, "All knowledge is in you." "What are you going to learn, my son?", the Veda asks. It is in you. "Yes, but I don't know." Remove the ignorance which exists, and knowledge is there.

Heart of the Lion

So this Occidental idea that I have to learn and take in knowledge as if I am ingesting water or food, you know, is crazy! Everything is in me. The universe is in me. What is the outside, is but a reflection of what is inside me. If I am happy, I see the world as a happy existence. A death in the family, and it seems the very willows are weeping, you see, the very clouds become dark, the world seems to weep with me. Is it not a fact? I project my inner feelings on my outer environment. One who is afraid sees the universe as a fearful place — all tooth and claw. One who is confident sees the world as a world of opportunity. One who is wise sees, like Shakespeare says, "Books in brooks, sermons in stones, knowledge in everything." For him everything speaks. For one who is the absolute knower, as Babuji Maharaj said, the question has the answer in it, not away from it, not outside it, not somewhere else. It is **in** the question. Probe deeper into the question and you find the answer within.

So you see our system of knowledge! There used to be a science called axionoetics. I don't know if many of you have heard that name. It is the knowledge of knowledge. Now, I consider it very crazy, you see, that I have to know about knowing before I can know. Then I must know about knowing about knowing about something before I can know — axionoetics of axionetics, you know, like parlour mirrors — infinite regression.

So let us stick to experience. Sahaj Marg says, "You don't need to know anything. You have to become something." When you become something, you will know what it is, by **being** that.

An unmarried boy, bachelor of sixteen, does not know what it is to be a father. He does not understand his father. He does not understand his mother. Why they behave in certain

The Purpose of Existence

ways, at certain times, towards him, and between themselves, too. He marries, he has a child — now he knows! Why his father behaved with him in certain ways; why his father loved him; why his father was also able to discipline him. Everything he understands — not by knowledge, but by the experience of being a father. One moment of time, and he knows everything about being a father.

So, to really know, become that which you wish to know. This has been the pursuit of saints, before they became saintly. Ramakrishna Paramahamsa lived as a woman for, I think, six months or one year — grew his hair, wore a *sari*, worked in the kitchen, washed clothes, washed vessels, slept with them, wept with them — everything with the women. To such an extent his emulation of the female life was perfect, that it is recorded that he even started menstruating. I don't believe that it is possible, but it is recorded as a fact in his biography. Which only means, that if you can be something totally, with all your heart — you don't have to go through these operations to change your sex — you can be what you want to be, at any precise moment.

This is how God comes to us — as a pig, as a fish, as the Garuda. Because, He just sits and thinks, "I am a bird," and He is a bird. And there He is, flapping his wings around, and then we think it's a helicopter, then we go and look — what is this strange bird? Even *rishis* have not been able to penetrate this. When Krishna comes as an uninvited boar, they don't know him. Only when they beat the boar, and they feel the beats, each one on his back, they say, "Oh, my God! We have beaten God Himself!" Our invited guest, our most respected guest, our Divine guest, for whom we have been waiting till midnight — He walks in, and I don't recognise him. Why?

Heart of the Lion

Because of my intellectual smallness, which says, "He must come as Krishna."

So the intellectual intellect limits! It makes my perceptions small. I look at the world through a keyhole. What do I really know? People look through microscopes at the minute, and through telescopes at the enormously big, but they only see this, nothing more. *Amoeba proteus* — wonderful! And they talk about its breeding habit — it doesn't breed, it just bifurcates. It's a happy life, no wife to bother about. When it wants to eat it just embraces what it wants to eat and engulfs it. Simple life, primordial life. Now that is one way of living. Cellular division — how does it happen? The scientists tell us very knowledgeably, "Oh, it just divides into two, you see." Yes, but why? Science does not tell us **why**, only **how**, and the **how** is not enough! If a man is satisfied **how** something happened, he is limiting his search for knowledge. **Why** does it happen? Why is one man able to sleep on a bed of nails, perfectly comfortable, as if he is on a Dunlop pillow mattress in an air conditioned room, with his beloved next to him stroking his head? And the other fellow, on a Dunlop pillow mattress in an air conditioned room with perhaps a bevy of beauties, is miserable.

Have we thought of this **why**? Science answers the **how**, spirituality answers the **why**. One answer. Not a multitude of answers to confuse us and confound us. One answer — samskara. Being in a palace, your samskara will not let you rest in peace, in comfort. Being in a hovel, his samskara permits him to sleep in the open, under the sky, enjoying Sirius, enjoying Arcturus, enjoying everything which we never even see often in our lives. "Oh, that looks like Venus." "No, no, but it's not a planet. It's a star." "What is the difference, Chari?" Then you start off, you see.

The Purpose of Existence

How — science. **Why** — spirituality. **What** — meditation. It is foolish to ask why I am here. I **am** here. Now let me find out where I have to go, and what I have to become. It is enough for me.

A millionaire does not want to become a billionaire just because he is a millionaire. Even a man who has nothing wants to be a billionaire, even the one who is in the red wants to be a billionaire. So the aspiration to be a millionaire or a billionaire is not restricted to the have-nots, it is there with the haves, and it is there with the have-much, too. Aspiration guides us.

In aspiration, we don't need to know what I am at this moment and why I am what I am at this moment. I have only to follow the call of my aspiration and keep going towards it, and I shall inevitably become that. Thank you.

Ashram Site Dedication, South Lenasia
April 18, 1993.

Dear brothers and sisters, today is a very auspicious occasion for the Mission in South Africa, and therefore for all of you, too. By the grace of my beloved Master, Babuji Maharaj, the Mission has its own ashram site, very kindly donated by Govindbhai and his family, as I announced some days back, and today at this first meditation, on behalf of all of you, I dedicate this property to Babuji Maharaj.

I think it is a sign of his immense grace and love for us that, in a sense, we start off with a bang with two marriages on the site! I pray that the couples may be blessed by Babuji Maharaj with felicity, with health, longevity, and a life full of happiness together, in the true tradition of all marriages — **"until death do us part."** I pray that all of you will bless them on this happy and auspicious occasion. May there be many more such auspicious and joyful occasions in the ashram that will be built here with the co-operation of all of you.

Everything needs a good beginning. I remember once, Babuji Maharaj asked me where I was going to do something. I gave him a plan, and he said, "How are you going to begin?" Because, as the English proverb says, "Well begun is half done." We have begun well, and I hope everything will reach a successful conclusion very shortly, because this will be your ashram — an ashram in South Africa for the people of South Africa, living in South Africa. A symbol of unity of all the people living here, people of all races, all colours, all religions, united under the spiritual umbrella of Sahaj Marg, and growing together harmoniously, marching towards the goal harmoniously, hand in hand, and making this land, which has been, in a sense, tortured by various problems over the past few centuries, shine in the glory of a united land, a united people, a united culture, united in spirituality. May it be so. Thank you.

Pitfalls of Spirituality
April 19, 1993

Some more information about Sahaj Marg which people have asked for, especially, problems in sadhana, pitfalls, etc. I think, like everything in Sahaj Marg, there is a situation of no problem, or a situation of too many problems. We always seem to swing between these extremes. Personally, I don't think the way itself has any problems. After all, it's a simple way — Sahaj Marg. It's a natural way, and we are supposed to have the help of the great Masters, who are really Masters of the path, Masters of the goal. People who can be Masters of our destiny. I mean Masters in every sense — Master.

I think the first pitfall we have to avoid is a misunderstanding of what this 'Master' means, because there are many people who come expecting miracles. Expecting, you know, all sorts of wonderful things — magic, instant transformation — thinking that the Master is going to do everything for us. I think that is the first big danger — not understanding what a Master is, and what is his relationship going to be with the abhyasis, with each *sadhak*. The word 'Master' really means, one who has mastered **himself**. It has nothing to do with mastery over powers of nature, mastery over this, that, and the other.

The other day I was seeing this movie, *King of Kings*, and there was a strange, what should I say, opposition of ideas when somebody asks Jesus to show a miracle. He refuses. At the same time he says, "If you have faith, you can move that mountain." Very strange way of putting things. Rather misleading, I thought. Those of you who have read Shakespeare, will remember the three witches and their predictions — that, "When Birnam Wood to Dunsinane Hill shall come." It is fulfilled in a very strange way, when people cut down the trees and they march under them. It looks as if the whole forest is marching!

So, I don't think you can really move a mountain, or make a forest come towards you, or anything like that. At the same time, we cannot say it is impossible, because when we say things are possible or impossible, we speak based on our experience, each one of us. And our experience is limited to our sensory experience — *pancha indriyas*, as we call them in Sanskrit. Smell, taste, touch, vision, feel. "*Shabda, sparsha, rasa, roopa, gandha,*" as they say in Sanskrit. We have no other experience. I think you can say that, excluding a very, very, very minute, minuscule minority, over the ages, human experience is limited to sensory experience.

So, to say that it is not possible, we are basing our statement on a ridiculously small level of experience, because it is well known that our senses are limited. We touch, and what we feel with our touch is extraordinarily ridiculous. We see, but the limit of our vision is a few thousand angstroms of what we call visible light. We cannot go beyond the violet at one end; we cannot go beyond the red at the other. In between, we see something, and we call this vision. We cannot hear much — even owls, bats, dogs — they are supposed to hear what we cannot hear.

So if you see the human being really, he is a ridiculously puny, stupid, incapable of experience sort of life form. Left to ourselves we have no experience at all. You see an ant. You put a bit of butter there, in half an hour the ants are there.

Pitfalls of Spirituality

They smell it. We cannot smell butter unless it is rancid. You try to put away — you know, in our villages we have what is called an *uri* in Tamil, which Krishna robs every time. Something which is made of ropes and suspended from the ceiling, on which the pots are kept — butter, sweets, fruit — and the ants can go from here, right up the wall, across the ceiling and come down the rope to that *uri*.

On the other side, much of our technological brilliance is perhaps due to our sensory limitations. We see with a telescope things which no animal or bird on earth can see. We are able to manipulate artificial fingers in atomic chambers by just putting a hand in a glove and doing this, and you manipulate enormous tongs somewhere, which is able to lift up radium, push back radium, all sorts of funny things. We are able to hear through hearing aids. So man's intelligence has been, his brilliance has been, in overcoming his sensory limitations. But we have restricted this, very stupidly, very foolishly to the material world. So, notwithstanding our brilliant technological inventions, discoveries, creations, yet when we are translated to the spiritual world, the scientist is as stupid as the non-scientist. He is for all practical purposes no more than a village idiot in spirituality, because he thinks his brilliance can only be expressed in the material life. The spiritual life he ignores, which means that his brilliance is only expressed in the material world, in the sensory world, and in none else.

So when it comes to understanding what a Master is, the brilliant scientist, brilliant technologist, they are as stupid as any village fool. At least the village fool says, "What can we say? It may be possible. For God, all things are possible." The intellectually brilliant fellow says, "Not at all. Where is God? Show me? I have probed the immensities of the universe with my telescopes on Mount Palomar, etc., and I am going to probe farther with my extraterrestrial telescopes. Hitherto, my range has been a few hundred thousand light years, a million light years perhaps, but now I am going to be able to go to the very edges of the universe." At the same time, he says, "The universe has no edge," because notwithstanding what Einstein said, the universe seems to be expanding at such a fast velocity, at least at the peripheral limits, that it goes beyond the velocity of light itself. Again the scientist is stumped. He says, "I can," and he says, "I can't." It is very much like the female mind — yes and no. Possible and not possible. The mind of the scientist is, par excellence, the mind of a woman! They don't know what they are talking about.

With all the immense body of accumulated knowledge over the ages, they still know nothing. You know, even such a stupid thing like Mars, and the so-called straight lines on it which they said at one stage, these are canals — even today nobody knows what they are. It's all speculation. So far, man has only been able to touch the surface of the moon. Two or three people have landed there. They have brought back some moon rocks and, unfortunately for our scientists, they are so ridiculously unimpressive. There is no difference between those rocks and our rocks. They are identical. Perhaps they contain more of some mineral than we are able to find, and less of something else than what we have but, by and large, it has been a scientific disappointment. Which makes us think, that if you were to go to another system, similar to the solar system, and to another moon there, perhaps it would be the same. But the scientist will not give up so easily. He has to go to Pluto, he has to go to Neptune and discover whether there is solid substance there, and whether it is the same as we have here.

Pitfalls of Spirituality

It is like a man who is going to woman after woman and finding the same things, and yet looking to see if there is not one woman who will satisfy him more than all the previous lineup of women. Womanizers, we call them. There is no difference, and there is a difference. What is the difference that is possible among a long lineup of women in a man's life? You know, some of them, I read yesterday in one of the newspapers or magazines, that before he is forty, the average American male has had at least twenty women in his life. And they don't seem to be any the wiser for it — they don't know any better after that. They have not found happiness with any of them, because if you have been happy you would not look for another one, you see, and yet a third, and yet a fourth, and the twentieth. Statistics have not revealed what happens at sixty. Whether the twenty has become sixty! It cannot shrink of course — I mean the number!

So what is it that brings a tangible difference in our perception? If, with all our magnificent extension of our sensory possibilities, we are no better than animals and birds and beasts, what is it that brings to human perception a certain dignity, a certain possibility which is not enjoyed by others. I cannot but say, or hazard an opinion, that it is only **love**. A man who loves his subject — certainly he sees more in it than a man who just approaches it with curiosity. The great scientists have all loved their subjects. The great lover has loved only one woman, not many women, you see, because love is not growing by accretion, by incremental levels. A man who has loved six women does not love his seventh more than he has loved the previous six, because of accumulated experience or accumulated loves. He only hates himself more and more. Increasingly diversified love outside makes you hate yourself more and more.

Heart of the Lion

So you see this funny thing, that the more we love the more we hate ourselves, therefore the less we love, perhaps the more we love ourselves. Perhaps this is the fundamental principle behind, let us say, spiritual love, which says, "One life, one Master, one Mission, one method." "Love Him who loves all." For Him to love all — no danger, because the 'all' is not broken up into the individual units comprising that 'all'. White light is not made up of violet, indigo, blue, green, yellow, orange, red, for the person who likes white. He does not say, "By jove, white is compounded of these seven colours of the spectrum. Let me love each colour individually!" No. He loves white, he wears white, white is purity. When it is split up it is impure.

So, one who loves all does not mean one who loves each person individually. Here comes the problem of spirituality, you see — "The Master loves me." I have always said, "No. The Master does not love anybody individually, cannot love anybody individually." It is like saying, "The Master loves white, therefore he loves red too, green too, violet too, indigo too." Not at all. For him, when the unitary principle is broken up it is no longer lovable. Otherwise he could have, you know, like the whirling dervishes, as they are called — Moulana Rumi's particular school of Sufis — the Mevlevis — he could have had them dress up in a big Arab dress, a *jellabah* with seven colours, so that when you whirl round you see them as white! Crazy, isn't it?

So, this fundamental problem of the Master: He is not **your** Master. He is himself a Master. This will remove all possibilities of misunderstanding, and also this need to be loved individually. "Oh, Master is love but he does not love me." Yes, and the sun shines, but it doesn't shine upon me when I am in the room. I have to expose myself there. The

Pitfalls of Spirituality

sun shines for everybody, black or white, Kwa-Zulu, Natal — everybody! It doesn't make any difference to it. The sun shines because it is its nature to shine.

The Master is a Master because his nature is one of mastery, mastery of himself first. In obedience to the ancient principle that he who is a Master of himself is a Master of the universe. Now, 'Master of the universe' does not mean that he is also Master of Pluto, Master of Neptune, Master of other galactic systems. It does not mean anything of that sort. Master of the universe — Christ said, "My kingdom is not of this world." People called him Master, too, in his lifetime. What was he Master of? "If thou art the Master can thou change this water into wine?" He said, "Tempt not thy Lord, thy God in vain."

Mastery is not in transmutation of metals, lead into gold. We leave that to the alchemists. It is not in changing a woman into a man, or vice versa, physically. We leave that to the surgeons. It is not in curing disease. We leave that to the doctors. It is not in spinning cotton into cloth. We leave that to the spinners and the weavers. Then, somebody says, "But what on earth am I here for? I want a Master!" Yes, of course you have one! "But then you say he's not my Master." Yes. Of course not. He is not automatically your Master. His Mastery can be used in enabling you to master yourself. How? By doing what he did. By obeying him in everything that he says. Therefore, first of all, you must want to be like him. Not a five foot, three inch man with a beard, with false teeth, looking very, you know, docile and cherubic! Not like that. Then you are insisting that your water must be in a triangular glass or a conical glass or in a pyramidal glass. I want water when I am thirsty. It doesn't matter what the glass is — it may be of gold, it may be of pewter.

Heart of the Lion

So you see, this first misunderstanding, the greatest misunderstanding, the most tragic misunderstanding, that I can go to a Master and find myself immediately, is the first and the greatest pitfall. "Oh, I have a Master. He will do everything for me." He will help you to do everything for yourself. He cannot do an iota for you by himself.

I am talking from experience. I have been very close to my Master, very intimate, and my statements are based on the authority of personal experience. I don't depend on dogma and on literature in spirituality. I depend on my experience. In my experience, Babuji Maharaj always said, "If you cannot co-operate, I cannot help." It was a very clear statement. Hundreds of times he has told sick people, "Go to the doctor!" Many more hundreds of times he has told people who had no jobs, "Find a job. Apply in the newspaper, you will find it." He did not raise his hand and say, "*Om, Krim-aim-swaha...*," and everybody became well, all daughters got married, sons got jobs, everything was hoity-toity. He never did it. Perhaps he could not do it. Perhaps he could do it but it was not permitted. Because, you know, there are cases where he tried to raise people up several points, and Lalaji from above rapped him on the head and said, "Stop this nonsense! You will destroy him."

So you see, the secret of his inability to do things for us was not **his** inability, but **our** inability to help him to do things on us which we are unable to stand. Even a stupid jeweler knows, you see, that gold is of such and such nature, lead is of such and such nature. You must know the metals with which you are working. You cannot use a blowtorch on diamonds — it will become carbon. The same for a chemist, but tragically very different for the person who has given the diamonds to be set.

Pitfalls of Spirituality

So you see, the Master is not limited by himself, or his capacities or his powers. He is limited by us. Each one of us is a different sort of limitation, or a concatenation of limitations, to him. One has affection, but will not practise. Another practises cleaning, but not meditation. Another meditates but says, "I don't need cleaning." The man who is very ardent in his practice has no affection for the guru. Those who practise according to the letter of the law do not obey his changed statements, on different occasions, under different circumstances. They say, "But Babuji, you have written in your own book." He says, "Aha. I have written." He could not say that, "I am the author of this, and I have a right to change what I have written!" He never said it, so this man went away thinking he has won a victory over Babuji, you see, a philosophical victory, maybe a victory of authorship — "You see, I have limited him to what he has written."

Here comes the misunderstanding that this written law is superior to the spoken law. Not at all. One speaks the law first, and then it is written down. Nothing was ever written before it was spoken. I am using the word *spoken* in its broadest meaning, that even when I speak, I am speaking with myself. I employ myself with a dissertation with myself, in an argument with myself, in a discussion with myself. When we evaluate what we call the pros and cons in our mind, that's what we are doing. I argue with myself, assuming the positions of this side and that side of the bar, so to speak. And then when I am clear in myself I write down things.

So a man who can use himself to be his own opposition and argue very strictly, very honestly with himself, will find the truth. So, when the Master says, "Notwithstanding what I have written, you are to do this now," we have to obey. So, reading the books, following the books, few of us do. If we have not that foundation of obedience at least to the written law, how are we going to obey the spoken law? He said, "No, no, Babuji, you see." Babuji says, "Intelligence is not necessary." People who don't want to pay fifteen dollars for a book find this argument very useful. Babuji said, "Not necessary. I have not passed beyond the fifth class." Yes, but Babuji did not own one million rand houses. He did not own Mercedes Benzes. He did not own immense stalls in the Johannesburg market from where people became millionaires on potatoes, bananas, chips, what have you.

So if you want to be like Babuji, you must be like Babuji in everything, not use that poor man only as an excuse to avoid paying fifty rands for a book! We are all hypocrites, we are cheats. But remember, you are a hypocrite towards yourself, and you are cheating yourself. You are lying to yourself. "No, no, Babuji did that." Yes, he ate half a *chapati* and a weak *dahl* — you have all eaten, I hope, some of you in Shahjahanpur — and a *subji*, so-called, which was a little stronger, thicker gruel with half a potato in it, or sometimes only a quarter of a potato. But your tables are laden with stuff — three different types of honey, four different types of jam, several types of butter, a variety of cheeses, white bread, yellow bread, blue bread, black bread, rye bread.

So which of you here is like Babuji, that you can afford the luxury of saying, "Babuji did not ask for intelligence."? You cannot. Are you willing to give up your money? Are you willing to give up your Mercedes Benzes and your million dollar houses? Then, talk of Master. Otherwise you are all awful liars. This is the second great pitfall. First — not knowing what a Master is — whether he can do anything for us. If so, how? Second — misusing that poor man, that

Pitfalls of Spirituality

enormously divine person as an excuse for all our stupidity, our fraud, our corruption, our greed, our acquisitiveness. How can he help? You tell him, "Babuji, you said intelligence is not necessary. I want simple people." Yes, but are you simple? Which one of you here can say, "Yes, I am simple." He lived on a pension of twenty-eight rupees a month, and he fed all of us, until I came into the picture and I insisted that abhyasis should pay a certain amount, at least for Basant. It took me four years to convince him to charge a small donation of thirty rupees per head! He said, "People cannot afford." I said, "If you can afford, they can surely afford." He said, "No, no, people from Sitapur will complain. See, poor fellows, they are paying six *annas* bus fare to come and go." I said, "People from south India are paying sixty rupees to come and go. If anybody is entitled to claim, they are entitled to, you know... Not these fellows from Sitapur who are living spitting distance away from you." It is like our abhyasis here — "Low Point not going to High Point; Laudium not going to Johannesburg; Venda not going anywhere!" All people in Mercedes Benzes, money in immense quantities in banks, but unwilling to spend, adding more and more and more, one day to die like a squirrel in winter, three inches above an enormous hoard of nuts that it has accumulated during summer, which it could not find in winter, which it did not know it had hidden.

Few of you rich people know where your money is today. Some people have so much money that they don't know where it is anymore. Squirrels are better. Poor things, they have not the knowledge of what they have acquired. But even in our acquisition there is no knowledge! You see what a travesty our life has become. Second great pitfall — do not misuse your Master. We don't know how to use him because we don't know what he is. But all the time we are misusing him, misquoting him, claiming to be his devotees, his *bhaktas* — second great pitfall.

Third great pitfall? "After all, he is a human being like us, sir. He is weak. You know, poor fellow, he cannot even bend and lift up his walking stick if it falls. At night somebody has to accompany him to the bathroom. He has false teeth. How can he help us?" I too, made that mistake — but only once, when I saw him for the first time. But when I saw his eyes, everything faded. He removed my ignorance. Otherwise, being a big strong fellow myself, pretending to be intelligent, pretending to be modern, Westernized, I would have gone the way of all the Western intellects — drugs and women, at least. At least drugs and women would have been my lot — in plenty. Fortunately, my first sight of him brought out all my foolishness. I said, "What is this person, lying like a bundle of clothes to be washed on the bed?" You know, he looked like a *dhobi's* bundle, as we say in India. And I was, metaphorically speaking, beating my forehead in self-disgust and saying, "What have I come here for, all this way from Madras to Shahjahanpur to see this person lying on this dirty bed?"

Many of you are still thinking like that, which is the tragedy. Nodding heads is no use — one must touch one's heart to find out what is the truth of this third pitfall — that, "I am better than him. I can walk farther than him. I can eat more than him. I can read better than him. I can understand everything which he cannot understand. I can digest cheese and butter but that person can't. I can sleep more than him. I have more money than he ever had. He has to come humbling himself and ask for donations. I never put out my hand for anything." How many of you don't feel that you are **obliging** your Master when you give your ten rands, and fifty

Pitfalls of Spirituality

rands, and hundred rands to the Mission ? Enormously big pitfall.

We have a saying in Tamil, that you make, you know, a *putli* of Ganesh — a figure of the Lord — and then when the time comes to offer *prasad*, you break off his hand or his leg and offer it as *prasad* to himself. This is what we are doing. Everything that we have comes from Him. The sunlight comes from Him. Our pleasure comes from Him; our pain comes from Him; our riches come from Him. But every time I have to put my hand into my pocket and bring out a donation, I think this is **my** money. And this is my common observation, that even when we give to a beggar, you know, immediately we look at a beggar, our sympathies overcome us, and we put our hand in, thinking, "I will give him everything I have in my purse!" We open it, touch a five rupee note, but pull out a quarter-rupee coin and give it to him. Similarly, when people come to give their, what it was called yesterday — commitment. No. Pledge! Pledge what? What have you that you can pledge? Is it yours? Today here, tomorrow gone forever. Who can pledge? Either you give now, or don't give now. No pledges. Who knows whether you will be here tomorrow to fulfil your pledge? Do you want the weight of a broken promise around your neck to bring you back into the next life? Beware of making pledges which you will not fulfil, which you don't intend fulfil, which you cannot possibly fulfil.

You see, there is a wealth of wisdom hidden in this saying of Master — "Now." Because **now** is the only moment I am sure of. Tomorrow I may not be here. I have already told you about the preceptor who told an abhyasi that he was very tired, and said, "Come back tomorrow." Babuji said, "Only God can say, 'Come back tomorrow'," because He, being eternal, knows he will be here tomorrow. He being God, and eternal, knows that the abhyasi will also be here tomorrow. **He** can say, "Come back tomorrow." This preceptor, even if the abhyasi is here tomorrow, does he know whether **he** will be here tomorrow to say, "Come to me tomorrow, I will give you a sitting." It is a commitment for the future, and if he does not fulfil it and dies before it is fulfilled, God help him!

So don't make commitments. Don't make pledges. Don't ask abhyasis to come tomorrow. Tell them, "I am not able to give you anything now. Sorry." But don't say, "Come tomorrow." It is a most dangerous promise to make. Don't tell the Master, "Tomorrow I will start meditation, when I go back to, I don't know, Lionsville, I will start cleaning." "When is that going to be?" "Well, I am here for three weeks in the heart clinic. Then, by your grace, if I am all right, I will go back to Lionsville, or Leopardsville or Pantherville. There I have been asked to rest for two weeks, for bed rest, by the Doctor. So, Babuji — five weeks, give me time. Then I will start cleaning and meditation." There is no heart attack which prevents a man from meditating today. In fact, he should meditate today if possible, if he is to overcome this heart attack and step into one of two paths. You know the famous experiment involving the particles of matter — they always follow a particular path. You open two paths and, for no reason, some go through this, some go through that. Nobody is able to say why. Perhaps they are also having hidden samskaras which guide them to this way or to that way!

If it is my destiny to die, I should die meditating. I remember a preceptor in our country in India who had a heart attack, and stopped meditation. Babuji was very upset. He said, "This man is so stupid. He is going to die. The best way of dying is to sit in meditation thinking of the Master when

Pitfalls of Spirituality

the door into eternity is opened automatically. Instead of that, he is not meditating, he is taking medicines and he is relying upon some fools, astrologers. What is this I am telling you?" These were Babuji's words.

Fourth pitfall — putting your faith in everything and everybody **except** the one you call Master." You see, we are all thinking of pitfalls such as immorality, vice, drunkenness, women for men, men for women, all these funny things. They are **nothing** compared to these big pitfalls. Do you mean to say a Master will not forgive your womanizing? Only, he says, "Don't call another man a sinner." Like Christ, when the adulteress was to be stoned, Jesus took up a stone and said, "Take. I give you the stone myself. Let him in whom there is no sin cast the first stone ," and they all turned around in shame and went away. The only sin we do which cannot be forgiven is to call other people sinners. Our sins don't exist — Babuji Maharaj has said, "The greatest sin is to **think** of sin." Sin is not in the action. Sin is in the thought, subsequently, which makes us feel guilty, brood over what we have done again and again, and because of that it becomes grosser and grosser and inevitably drives us in the same way to the same sin, again and again — each time it becomes stronger and stronger.

Like a man who takes his boss's money, maybe ten rand, you see, to play the horses the first time. He loses it. Next Saturday he takes twenty rand, hoping to double it, put back the ten plus twenty, thirty rand, and keep ten for himself. In no time at all he owes his company several hundred thousand rand. The more he loses, the more he thinks he can win the next time. This is a fact of the psychology of gamblers, you see, and some of them are so stupid, they start speaking in terms of statistical law! "There has been a run of bad luck, so now the next throw of the dice must give me good luck." The run can go on infinitely because statistics says that, given a sufficiently large number, half and half is the result. But for me, my whole life may be spent in getting the no-show sign all the time, and the next one who comes there when I am dead and carried away will be the first man to draw my profit!

So we are basing our claims, or our hopes of success, on chance, on friends, on assumptions, but not on love, faith, and hope. It's all pitfalls. "No, no. Babuji says you may live only three years." Babuji never said — I mean, let us assume, you see, he said so, because he could not say. He says, "Don't go to the doctor. I can remove this in three sittings." "But sir, what to do? You know, my wife says, 'Don't be stupid.' My father says, 'What? Guru for medicine? Keep your guru for spirituality.'" See, we have got compartmentalized minds. For good cooking, well-washed clothes — the wife. For pleasures — another woman. For companionship — a third who has an intellectual mind and can talk and dissert on so many subjects and keep us company intellectually speaking. A fourth to accompany me to the restaurant because she is good to show off — nice hair-do, good dresses, good clothes sense, and hangs well on my arm like my jacket hangs well on me! So you see, we have compartmentalized minds. Love, instead of including everything, has become now, that which is not in anything else. Not even in the Master. So I would like to tell you that these material pitfalls into which everybody can slip anytime, but for the help of God — because they are in your samskaras, they are pushing you inevitably, inexorably towards that particular pit — only the Master can save you by removing that samskara. But we don't go to him. We try to build fences, and a man comes and jumps over the fence. We build a wall, another climbs over

Pitfalls of Spirituality

the wall and jumps, just to see what is on the other side of the wall. Something which is so carefully protected must have something wonderful inside. Isn't it?

So forget these sensory pitfalls, worldly pitfalls. These are everybody's cup of poison, cup of misfortune. There is relief, but only from and through the Master. He can help us by cleaning off all our tendencies, our samskaras, so that these pitfalls are as if they have been filled up with sand, and no more in my path. But the big pitfalls — the pitfall of misunderstanding, the pitfall of wrong expectations — these are the **real** pitfalls which block our path, which make progress impossible. Not because **he** is helpless, but because **we** are helpless.

So, please try to understand spirituality properly. What is a Master? Why is he **my** Master? It is not because I am his slave. The Western people rebel at this idea, you see, that because he is my Master, I must be his slave. "I don't want to be anybody's slave. I am a great man myself. I am the chairman of, I don't know, the Federal Bank of Johannesburg. Or I own De Beers, so why do I need a Master?" You need a Master precisely because there are things in you — you may be the best diamond miner yourself, but he can mine something from inside you — the dirtiest things which are lying hidden, which are not accessible to anybody, not even to yourself, after removing which you are richer than if you have all the diamonds of this world with you. Here, it is by un-becoming, un-doing.

In Sahaj Marg the world is not to become something. We un-become until we are what we were. It is like a person undressing to expose his naked self which is as he was born with. To do this, it is like cleaning the sewers. You have a special class of people who come to clean your sewers, who are willing to go down into that muck, into that stink, and clean it for you. That is why Babuji said, "I am really in the sewers and gutters of humanity." Imagine what a person must be capable of — what suffering, what fortitude, what courage, what bravery, that he goes into this hellhole of existence and comes out clean — not only clean himself, but cleaning you also in the process. Are we or are we not going to accept such a person's service? If we are, do we know what service he is really doing for us? If we appreciate that, is there a price that we can pay which can ever be too much for the service he is rendering? Can it evaluated in terms of rands?

Therefore, when the Devil tempted Christ, when it tempted Buddha — everybody is tempted at the final levels, you see — and said, "I give you dominion over all this world," they laughed. They said, "Keep it. You are the Devil, you need it. I don't." Automatically this should make us think, that with all my possessions, with my gilded securities, with my gold, with my diamonds, with my amber, am I going towards the Devil? Or am I going towards the other end? And if in going towards this end, these are going to be a bar to my advancement and my progress, is it not better to give it away?

A donation is not a donation to the Master or the Mission. You are ridding yourself of some of this enormous weight that you have tied around your necks. You should be grateful to a man who asks you for your money, and say, "Take. What I would not give myself, I am giving you when you ask, because so many kilos of gold I have lost today, and therefore so much lighter I am." In all my sixty-five years of life I have known only one man who ever did this, and strangely he was a Purohit. You know, people used to give him four *annas*, eight *annas*. My father once gave him a hun-

Pitfalls of Spirituality

dred rupees, because we knew he was suffering. He returned the money, weeping. He said, "Don't give me this money. It is a burden I will have to bear. I will be tempted. I will be sullied. My practice will be destroyed. I will start expecting. Please don't do me this dis-service." And I am happy to say my father felt a sense of shame and took back the money.

Giving is not easy. Taking is even more difficult. Which of you will take from me ten rands if I give it to you? "*Nahi, nahi*, Chari Saheb! I don't need it. You know, I have got so much. *Aap rakhiye*. Thy need is greater than mine." To give is easy. To receive — much more difficult. Which of you will accept help unless you pay for it. Why are you so proud that you are not going to a cheap doctor but to a very expensive doctor? Because you think your life is worth more. "No, no, I paid a hundred thousand rand for my medical treatment. He only paid twenty-six thousand." Why are men so happy when they go to expensive prostitutes? I know a man who retired from the army, who had been quite a close friend of my family. He himself told me that when he was discharged in Jammu, in the northern province of Jammu, he called his henchmen that they have — two *sepoy*s. He said, "Find out who is the most expensive prostitute in town." And he went there. I said, "What did you get?" He said, "Nothing! But you know, it was just a fling." I said, "Did you find pleasure in the woman, or pleasure in throwing away your money?" He said, "Pleasure in throwing away my money, as I realised later. The woman is always the same." So the rich man finds pleasure, not in using money, but in throwing money, thinking that the more he throws the greater he is. But unfortunately, always for the wrong things, for his sicknesses, for his pleasures, for his fun, for his holidays, but not for anything which can help him one step up the ladder of spiritual evolution.

Heart of the Lion

"Give thy all, and come with me," Christ said. So has every great saint except my Master. He said, "Here, you don't have to give me anything except the rottenness in you, the filth in you, the slime in you. Throw all this out, I will take it." When has a Master in the history of humanity ever asked you for your rubbish, saying, "You keep your happiness, your gold to yourself, my friend." Implying that such gold and such health as you have are given by Him! So can we offer to God what is God's? "Render unto Caesar what is Caesar's ," because you have taken from him. From me, you cannot take what I cannot give. That's what the Master implies, you see, and having given, as one proverb says, "Only a dog eats its own vomit." The giver does not ever take back.

Therefore you must consider it a privilege to be able to support his work with your body, with your mind, with your wealth, with your capacities — not think of it as another act of petty robbery, and smile to yourself when you have got away with two hundred rand and think, "No, no. I have fooled him this time. Next time, better luck. You know, he doesn't really know the value of the rand. Two hundred rand for him is a big thing. After all, he is a poor man living in Shajahanpur, filth."

Biggest, most potent, most destructive pitfall on the way is the lack of right understanding of the Master, and adding to it, the wrong understanding of the Master which you think is right, which makes you think you can bribe him, you can fool him, you can cheat him into giving you what you want, very much like we do in our businesses. This is not a business place. Here, the boss cannot be cheated. He cannot be fooled. He may tolerate, you see, what you are doing. That is His greatness, His love, His mercy.

Pitfalls of Spirituality

Let us also remember that we have given too much attention, perhaps, to the material pitfalls — old age, sickness, vicious temperament, attachment to lusts — these are petty things. Two thousand years ago Christ said, "Let him in whom there is no sin cast the first stone." It was quite, you know, clear that everybody was sinning. At least fifteen hundred years before him, Buddha said the same thing.

Here in Sahaj Marg, there is no sin, there is no virtue. What we think of as sin becomes our sin, and the only way to avoid it is to make a resolution, which he calls a repentance, saying, "I shall sin no more." There is no need for forgiveness because I forgive myself. There is no need for retribution because I am always punishing myself. Who is the God who is punishing me? Who is the God who is saving me? I save myself. I punish myself. I destroy myself. I alone can recreate myself, but I need His help to show me how to do it — therefore the Master. Thank you.

Love Thy Neighbour As Thyself
April 23, 1993

Many questions keep coming up. The same questions from different people, different questions from the same people, and I think one of the benefits of staying in a place for a long time, two weeks, is to get out, or bring out all the problems — personal problems, world problems, cosmic problems, problems of abhyasis, problems of preceptors. We seem to be having so many problems. Babuji Maharaj said, "One who has one goal has only one problem — how to get there." But people have many goals, so they have many problems. I mean, this is a matter for common sense, that if I want to go at the same time to Durban and to Capetown, I can't. If also I want to go to Harare I have three problems, now — Where to go. How to get there? So the one way, one infallible way, of reducing our problems is to reduce our aspirations to just the one single aspiration of evolution to the highest. When you are not able to do that you have to struggle, because you give equal importance to all goals, or sometimes foolishly, you give more importance to lesser goals and less importance to the higher goals.

Now, several thoughts I have been having, you know, because I have been talking to Dr. Mukund and our abhyasis at breakfast. One thought came to me during meditation this morning. The Christian advice, or directive, "Love thy neighbour as thyself." We all say it's impossible. But the crucial word there is 'as thyself.' Why did not Christ just say, "Love thy neighbour," and stop? It was good enough to say,

"Love thy neighbour. Love the blacks like thy neighbour. Love the whites." Why did he add the words 'as thyself'? Because we cannot love anybody more than we love ourselves. And if we hate ourselves we can only hate. No human being can do to others anything more than what he can do to himself. So when we hate, we project hate on everybody, and then we misunderstand his quotation and say, "Love thy neighbour as thyself? But Chari, it's not possible! How can I love my neighbour? I can't even love my wife. I can't even love my children. I can't even love myself!" Now here, this loving thyself is not in the narcissistic sense, but in the way of loving my Self. You know, if I am to love myself I must know I have a Self. One who does not know he has a Self, or she has a Self, how can he or she love the Self?

So the first need is to recognize that we have a Self inside us which we have to learn to love. Now we love the ego — the lower self. We are attracted by the lower self because it pulls us in various directions which we call pleasure, satisfaction, success — the three goals today of humanity. Pleasure, satisfaction, success.

Spirituality does not recognize pleasure as a goal. Because, you see, in the whole of the animal kingdom there is no such thing as pleasure. "Aha, but what about animals mating?" Not for pleasure. A bull doesn't go around looking for a female. Instinct drives it. Honey badger going for honey — yes, but that is its food, it does not know that it is sweet. Lion killing a lamb — it does not know the difference between a lamb and a buffalo. It picks out what it can kill, kills it and eats it. So in the animal kingdom there is no pleasure even in sex, you see, even in mating. It is an instinctual drive. The idea of pleasure and pain comes only in the human existence, and today if you see society, all of our

Love Thy Neighbour As Thyself

efforts are towards maximizing pleasure and minimizing pain.

So you have so many things for maximization of pleasure, including chemicals which can increase your sexual potency, for instance. And so many things for minimizing your pain, such as tranquilizers. So what are we doing with our life? There should be a balance between pain and pleasure. Ideally it should be so balanced that there is no pleasure, no pain, like a no-profit, no-loss situation, which is very good. Because if you have profit, there is the possibility of loss. The more the profit the greater the loss, and of course, all businessmen tell lies. They say, "Oh, last year I suffered a loss of three million rand." What he has really lost is profit! Instead of seventeen million rand in the previous year he makes fourteen million rand this year, and he says, "I have lost three million rand!", and a gullible fellow like one of us here, you know, believes he has lost three million rand, when all that he has had is a reduction in his profit. Because when a businessman really loses money, most of them commit suicide! So until a businessman commits suicide, you know he is telling lies. For him, the suicide, the act of suicide is a truth, that today I have *really* lost.

Lies, lies, lies. And Christ asks again — you see, I am fascinated with his teachings — "What shall a man profit if he gains the whole world but loses his own soul." Now, why do we not know the value of our soul? Because as I said, we do not know we have a Self. If I have a Self, I would learn to at least have some sort of connection with it, life with it, respect it, love it, and then if I can love the Self, then it is possible to come to the stage of, "Love thy neighbour as thy Self."

So you see, we don't know we have a soul. In fact, from the middle ages the so-called occultists, the so-called people of Paracelsus and his tribe, the people who have been delving into things like, you know, transmutation of metals into gold — the alchemists — they have gone to every extent to find out if there is such a thing as a soul or life, even to the extent of weighing a corpse just after a man dies, to see if there is any difference in weight. Even there, though there has been some modicum of search, it has been a materialistic search, thinking that the soul is a material stuff, which must have a weight, which must have a form, which must have attributes. So you see, even the wise people, the philosophers, the alchemists, the occultists, they have thought of the soul as something material which is inhabiting me which leaves at the time of my death, and therefore will contribute to a reduction in the weight of what is left behind, and when they don't find it, they say, "No soul! If there is no loss in weight, how can there be something which has gone out?"

So you see, this material idea is so pervasive that even the soul is thought of as something material, something which can be killed, something which can die. But the Gita says, "It is never born. It never dies." The Vedas speak of it as something which water cannot wet, which fire cannot burn, which the wind cannot blow away, because there is nothing there which can be affected by these elements. If that is so, then what is this suffering that we are talking about? Can the soul suffer? Because you cannot suffer unless you are to be affected by the elements — earth, water, fire, air, ether — whatever we want to call them. "*Shabda, sparsha, rasa, roopa, gandha,*" as I said the other day. If they cannot affect the soul, then what is all this suffering about?

Love Thy Neighbour As Thyself

Therefore, we have to come to this derived logic that only that which can be affected by these elements, by these senses, suffers or enjoys. If that is so, for a dead one there is no suffering, there is no enjoyment. Q.E.D.- There can be no heaven, there can be no hell. Because heaven and hell are described as places of utter suffering or of absolute enjoyment. So where is enjoyment, where is pleasure for the dead? Neither exists. For the saint, it doesn't affect him at all, because death for the average human being is the ultimate pain, the ultimate loss, the ultimate tragedy. But the saint dies every moment — when he sits in meditation he is lost! He is dead to this world, therefore — 'living dead'. His body may suffer. His body may speak. His body may shout out to God, "Why hast thou forsaken me?", but he doesn't shout. He is in the calm of his absolute meditation, what we call the *mahasamadhi*. The body speaks, it works, it runs, it mates, it defecates, it does all these things because it is the body. The soul, in its utter state of weightlessness, state of nothingness — suffers nothing, enjoys nothing, feels nothing, knows nothing, sees nothing.

Therefore, you see, we have to really understand what is spirituality. We have to really understand or try to find what is this soul in me, which I call my **Self**. If I know that it exists, I have to learn to love it more than I love myself — not my Self, but myself! I love myself, you know, narcissistic love — gazing into the pool and looking at my eyes and my nose, you know, and thinking, "I am beautiful. I am desirable. I am attractive. I am rich. I am wise." When the soul says, "You are nothing, because I am nothing. I am in you, and I am the motor which is driving you. If I fail, you drop dead. If I leave you, you can be possessed by the Devil!" How can the Devil possess us? If it is not something which is coming into me and running me from inside, pushing my Self

Heart of the Lion

to the other side because I have never recognized that Self, the existence of that Self. I have never had confidence in it because I don't know it is there. I am like a child, terror-stricken to be alone, shouting, "Mama! Mama!" And the mother comes in from the kitchen and says, "Darling, I'm here!" "Yes, but mommy, why did you leave me? I am so frightened." "Yes, but darling, don't you know I am in the kitchen? Didn't you hear the noise of the pots and pans?"

So we are like children, you see — lost, bewildered, frightened, miserable. Why? Because what is inside, we are seeking outside. We look for friendship outside. All friends are betrayers. Every man is betrayed by his **friend**. Enemies do not betray us. Enemies are after us all our lives. How can they betray? So the betrayal always comes from the innermost circle. It's not surprising that one of the twelve put Jesus Christ on the cross. Nobody else could have done it. The Romans would have slaughtered him, the Jews would have murdered him, but the betrayal comes only from the innermost circle, always. So beware of the innermost circle. We are afraid of the outermost circle. We are afraid of Soweto when we should be afraid of Lenasia. We are afraid of Lenasia 5 when we should be afraid of Lenasia 3. We are afraid of Lenasia 3 when I should be afraid of 190 Rose Avenue, because that is my ultimate *kabristan* (cemetery), my home is my *kabristan*.

We are afraid of graves and graveyards, forgetting that my bed is going to be my grave. In it I am going to die. You know that story of the man who was ferried across a river by a girl. He was a wise man, supposed to be a wise man among wise men, and he asked the girl, "Are you not frightened of this ferry business?" She said, "My lord, I have to earn my living. This is how I do it." "Yes, but my dear, it is so dan-

Love Thy Neighbour As Thyself

gerous. What happens when the wind blows and the river gets rough?" She says, "It can be dangerous, yes." "How did your father die?" "He died in a storm." "And your grandfather?" "He died in a storm, too. We have all died in storms in this river." So the wise man says, "Are you not afraid then, of ferrying this boat across the river?" She says, "Father, forgive me. How did your father die?" "Oh, he died at home peacefully in bed." "And your grandfather?" "He too died peacefully at home in bed." And she said, "Are you not afraid of sleeping in your bed at home?" (laughter)

So you see, we should be afraid of our beds, because that is where most of us are going to die. We should be afraid of our homes, but on the contrary, a good man in a good hospital under good attendants says, "Please take me home. I want to die at home." What on earth for? It is not **where** you die which matters, it is **how** you die which matters. How you die does not mean by sickness or in health, or heart attack or accident. The way in which my Self leaves this lower self, gets out of its cage which is a prison for it, and says, "Today I am free." Is that freedom real, or ephemeral, imaginary. If it is real, it is liberation. If it is not, it is a momentary freedom, like Babuji has described — a prisoner being let out, even from the dungeon for one hour a day, up into the sunlight for exercise, and after the one hour is over he goes back. For the bulk of humanity, death is such an escape — a moment of exercise in the sunlight of His benign presence, where we are told, "Think over what you did, which has brought about your incarceration here." If he is wise he will think over it, he will repent, he will be free. If he is arrogant and says, "*Thik hai!* Twenty years here or there, what does it matter?", he goes back in and he stays in.

Heart of the Lion

So it is **how** we die that matters, not **where** we die. Kings die in their palaces, beggars die in their, I don't know, hovels. The sick die in hospitals, the miserable die in their misery. They all go to the same destination. Now, many people imagine that there are more — there's a bigger population in hell than in heaven, but Babuji told me it is wrong. There are fewer souls in hell, thank heavens.

He told me a story of a long queue at the doors of Heaven, at the gates of Heaven, waiting there for days, millions of people lined up. Each one has to come and report to the receptionist, have his identity checked, and sent in to Heaven. Suddenly a vehicle draws up and there is a big flurry, you see, telephones operating everywhere, bells clanging, the gates opening. They are led in through a wicket gate one by one, normally. But the gates of Heaven are opened, and a car comes from inside. Bugles, fanfare, and this fellow is driven up, he is put into the car and driven there, when all these people are waiting for weeks, months. One fellow there, you know, must have been a Communist while on earth. Eventually when he reaches the, what we call the *sannidhanam* of Heaven, the grand audience chamber of God, he says, "My Lord, I have to make a complaint." The Lord says, "Yes? Even here? Even in my Divine presence there is a complaint? Yes, speak, my son." He says, "Lord, I waited eighteen days at your door. We were let in one by one. Eighteen days outside Heaven — you know it is like Hell. When you are not in Heaven you are in Hell." "Yes, what is your complaint?" He says, "Suddenly a car came up, your authorities from the gatehouse telephoned, there was a big flurry of activity, the gates were opened for this fellow, your Divine car came and took him in with much fanfare and bugles. I object to this nepotism, this favouritism." God smiled. He said, "In a way, you are right. But remember, my

Love Thy Neighbour As Thyself

son, people like you come in the millions every day to Heaven. A soul like that comes once in many millions of years. Don't you think he deserves a little special attention?" That was a rich man, who was a great man on earth. Such people come very rarely. "Even a camel may walk through the eye of a needle, but a rich man shall not enter the gates of Heaven. But this man made it, you see. Therefore, a little extra attention, a little recognition of the fact that even such a soul can come into my Divine presence."

So you see at the same time the rarity of such a soul going to Heaven, and also the multitudes of simple, innocent people who reach Heaven without any effort. Therefore Heaven is the more populous, not Hell. Unfortunately we are taught otherwise. We are told that Hell is full of people — even some wise people are said to have remarked, "Oh, I will have better company there!" — I mean in Hell. "My old drinking partners, my card playing partners, my gambling partners, my drug addict partners, etc., etc., etc. They will all be there. What will I do in a Heaven of fools, of simple-minded folk who don't know the difference between a rand and a rum, for instance?"

So you see, until we come to this idea that I have a Self, which is not myself, until I learn to love the Self, and not myself, until I learn to love my Self, not myself — how can I love my neighbour as my **Self**? It is impossible. What I am trying to say is, until we become spiritual and recognize the Self inside and learn to love it, to support it, to encourage it, finally to surrender to it, no one of us can love another person at all. It is all a lie, a cheat, a sham. Every time a man says, "I love my wife," I pity him. More, I pity her. And every time she says, "I love my husband," I pity her too. Nobody loves a husband or a wife. This is based on the truth of the Upanishads. There is a famous Upanishad, where Yagnavalkya is talking to his spiritual wife. She wants to be taught. "What is this you are speaking of so much — the Self, the Self. What is this Self?" He says, "My dear, the husband does not love the wife for the sake of the wife, but for the sake of himself — it is selfish." So you love yourself, and for your self's sake you think you love your wife. All that you want from her is the conveniences she affords you, in bed and out of it. What does she want? Money for her cosmetics, for her dresses, to go in a Mercedes car, to be a social butterfly. Without him it is not possible, so she needs him. It is a symbiotic relationship, each leeching on the other in their own way. Yagnavalkya said, "The wife does not love the husband for the sake of the husband, my dear, but for the sake of herself." So he wanted to, you know, balance the male and the female, because if he had just stopped with saying, "The husband does not love the wife for the sake of the wife," she would have thought all men are cruel, selfish, inhuman tyrants. He made it clear to her that it is the same story with the wife. It is the same story *vis-a-vis* the father and the son, the mother and the daughter, of everything.

Then a boy disciple comes and says, "What is this Self you are speaking about? What is this life?" He says, "Go to that tree, that big enormous ficus tree you see there." "Yes Lord, I see it." "Bring one fruit." He brings. He says, "Cut it open." "Yes my Lord, cut open." "What do you see?" "A lot of pulp and some seeds." "Take out a seed. Cut it. What do you see?" "Nothing." He says, "From that nothing, this immense tree has come!" Similarly, from the nothing in you, this immense thing that you think of as yourself has come. If that nothing is not there, you are not there.

Love Thy Neighbour As Thyself

So you see how many aspects, facets of wisdom, about this nothingness. And yet we say, "Oh, my Self is nothing." It is possible to say 'nothing' in two ways. It is nothing, but everything. Money which is nothing, really speaking, because the rupee I cannot use here, the rand you cannot use in India. You have to convert it. That is why there is so much talk about convertibility of currencies in your newspapers. What was six roubles to the dollar barely a year ago, I am told is something like one thousand roubles a dollar today, and I don't know where it will end up. I asked my friend Dmitri, who is in Madras, "What is the current rate of exchange?" He said, "I don't know, because even if I telephone and find out, by this evening it can be different!"

What is **our** currency worth? If I am dealing with that which is perishable, which will rot, which will burn under the fire or be buried for the worms to eat, I am dealing with a currency which is not convertible at all. Nobody in creation will buy my body for anything more than its value in flesh. Portia — pound of flesh. Who can take a pound of flesh? That miserly Jew fails. "Not more, not less by a hair's weight shall you take it out." So, what is the value of this body, which will perish in fire, which will rot if it is not buried, which the birds eat up, or the worms eat up. You know, the graveyard scene in *Hamlet*.

So what is it in me that is eternally of value, convertible wherever I go, acceptable wherever I go — like a wise man has a silver or a gold chain around his neck, because money falls in value — gold never falls in value — today's marketplace, you get today's market price. It is my soul. It is **that** which goes to Heaven, not my body. What we call in Tamil, "*Koondodu Kailasam*" — going to Kailasam with my *koondu*, which is the cage, you see, it's not possible. No bird can fly free **with** its cage. Can you throw the cage into the air with the parrot in it and say, "You are free. Fly away." It will think, "What a foolish Master I had all this life. All he has to do is to open a tiny door in it and let me fly away, and he is throwing me up with my cage, me in it." Is it possible? No, but we want it! Tradition speaks of saints who have disappeared with their bodies, the body is no more there. Stupid! For the vulgar, for the, you know, ignorant. They go to their shrines and say, "You know, he went up with his body." Where? Where can the body go? Up? It can only go down, and that is where most of our bodies take us — down and down and down.

So, how much respect should I have for my body? How much should I love it? How much should I look after it? The Isha Upanishad speaks of the body being like a chariot. Five horses, five pairs of reins, a charioteer, and the Master sitting in it. He says, "These five senses are the five pairs of horses. The charioteer is the mind. The reins are the subtle senses. The wheels, what takes me on the way. The Master sitting inside the soul." Now, the charioteer must have instructions from the Master — "Drive slowly, drive fast, drive to the left, drive to the right, rein in your horses," and when he gets to the destination the chariot is finished. Its purpose is over.

So for the purpose of my journey from here to there, I need a well-maintained vehicle, performance-wise. But we hear of emperors who have, you know, gold wheels on their chariots, diamond-studded harness round their horses, perhaps reins of human skin, well tanned, I don't know. Maybe Caligula had such a chariot — silver spikes, golden spikes. What happened to him? What happened to Genghis Khan? What happened to Hitler? What happened to Napoleon? What happened to Mussolini? The great Stalin, the great

Love Thy Neighbour As Thyself

Lenin, the great Brezhnev — where are they? The great pharaohs, where are they? People are hunting for their gold even today.

Two days back, I read in the paper that there's a secret chamber in the pyramid of Cheops which they have discovered, and they expect that there are treasures in it far beyond the treasures of Tutankhamen. What are we hunting for when we dig into the graves of the history of the past? Their treasures. Not for their wisdom, not for their lives. When we see the mummies of those pharaohs in their glass cases in the Egyptian museum at Cairo we are nauseated — at least I was. What is their destiny, what is their fate? To lie in their, you know, cases of empty skin, putrefaction being prevented by daily doses of injection of chemicals, to be gazed on by the vulgar, when in his lifetime you could not even look at him. One does not look at God. So that is the destiny of pharaohs, that is the destiny of all of us. As I always say, whether you are a rich man or a king or a prostitute or a poor man, the body will burn on the same funeral pyre. Some may have some sandalwood, some may have just ordinary wood, but burn the body must. So how much attention should we give to it? Minimum. Keep it healthy so that it does not betray me on the way. It should not drop dead before I finish my journey. A car must not stop on the way. It can be dangerous. In any case, I cannot reach my destination.

So you see, minimum attention to the body, maximum attention to the Self, which we call the soul. Enough money during the times of work when I can earn, apportioning the time and saying, "In this time, whatever I earn is mine." It may be billions, it may be millions, it may be few tens of hundreds, it does not matter. After all, if a potter is sitting at his wheel, he can only turn out so many pots per hour. No woman can have more than a child a year. If it is twins, two. If it is triplets, three. Not sixteen, not twenty-seven. So, wisdom decrees that I shall give equal attention to my material as to my spiritual life, because in this human embodied existence I **need** my body. Needing it, I must know how to use it wisely. What is wisdom in the usage of the body? For pleasure? No. Pleasure is incidental, as pain is incidental. A clock, to work properly the pendulum must tick between the two opposites — tick-tock, tick-tock. It cannot be very silent and in the middle, motionless. If it is to run the clock, it cannot.

So, human life swings between the opposites. It may be a violent swing between two extreme opposites, or it may be a gentle swing, just enough to keep the clock moving. If that much motion is there, if that much activity is there, the swing between the opposites is minimized until I don't know even the difference between pleasure and pain. It is only at the extremes that the differences are perceptible. If it is only going to swing one centimetre this way, and one centimetre that way, it becomes a notional difference. Now what is pain, and what is pleasure?

So to the saint, there is no pleasure, there is no pain, or sometimes you can even say pleasure is a pain, and pain is pleasure. When can we achieve this state where something is neither a pleasure nor a pain? Only when I don't swing more than is necessary to keep my internal clock ticking. I don't have to swing one mile this way and one mile that way, you see — then I really feel the extremes — extreme pleasure, extreme pain. But if it is just like this, you know (makes small gesture back and forth), you cannot even say what is pleasure, what is pain any more. There is only feeling, and the feeling is not of pleasure or pain, because it is not any more interpreted by my brain. Pleasure and pain are, after all,

Love Thy Neighbour As Thyself

interpretations of my brain. I feel something — my mind tells me that this is pleasurable, or that it is painful. If I did not have a mind, I would not know the difference between pleasure and pain. When you poke a needle into a man who is in deep coma, he doesn't feel it. You can cut away a chunk of his flesh, he won't feel it. So what happens to pleasure and pain? It is the nervous system, and when these swings are so minimal, like any anatomist or neurologist can tell you, there needs to be a minimum potential in any input, sensory input, before it can be felt. There must be enough in it to jump across the synapses, as they call them, for it to be transmitted upwards to the brain. If not, it will stop. The first gate will stop it.

So it is not necessary to go into a coma to stop pain or pleasure. If your swings are so minimal, your nervous system will take care of it. No jumps across the synapses, the neurons are fulfilling their duty. It is like a gate through which only one man can pass at a time — no mob, the mob is outside! I am serene in my inner self, one man coming in at a time. No danger, no problems of admission — this is discipline, you see. So when I discipline my swings between pleasure and pain, and minimize it so that only bare existential phenomenon are there, I have disciplined my nervous system, I have disciplined my mind. There is no more pain or pleasure for me, there is only existence — *sat*. What makes that possible is that minimal level of consciousness which I must retain to be in this world — *chit*. What I experience is utter bliss, because now I am free of pain and pleasure and I know that I am in a transcendental state, where neither pain nor pleasure intrude into my existence, but only the state of being, which is called *anand*. *Sat, chit, anand*.

Heart of the Lion

The fool who wants to enjoy **will** suffer because the pendulum **must** swing to the opposite. Otherwise life cannot be there. Perhaps that is why some people, at the point of extreme pleasure have heart attacks and die. A man dying when he gets a million rand lottery, or at the point of orgasm, falling dead. The bees are supposed to die like that, you know. In their mating dance the worker bees fly higher and higher, until finally the chosen one is up there. In the act of mating, he is cut off — he falls dead. His purpose is fulfilled. The next generation, the seeds of the next generation have been sown. What else is he there for now? Not to sow again and again and again and again and again and again, you see, ad nauseam — like human beings are doing.

You know, Bernard Shaw is supposed to have said that only two things in creation have no mating season — the donkey and the human being. And it is true — for them there is no mating season! Anytime is mating time. Day, night, it does not matter. Black, white, it does not matter. Male, female even, today it does not matter. We enjoy the distinction of being linked with the donkey as the only other thing in creation which has no mating season. Everything else obeys the law. We have no law. We have become lawless, obscene, miserable, filthy, dirty — excrements of nature. Why? Because of the swing, you know! The more we experience pain, the more we want to go towards pleasure, so we swing up. It's like the swing, you know, which children activate — vroom, vroom, they are going up and down, you know, and it becomes dangerous. Suddenly they don't know how to stop. They try to jump off and the swing hits them in the back, and they are cases for the hospital. You can see this in every house in Gujarat where they have swings, and in Tamil Nadu where we have swings. The children go crazy on a swing. Therefore an adult must be there. The more they swing this way, the more they swing that way. It is inevitable. It's a law of nature. More pleasure, more going towards health, more going towards wealth, the more I shall inevitably swing towards pain and ill health and poverty. It is as inevitable as night and day.

How to stop? Well, sit and gently relax, because the swing is there to be swung. Just a gentle movement, enough to keep the breeze. After all, the swing is there for the purpose that instead of using a fan to fan me, I swing to make the relative motion of the air possible around me. It is only for that purpose. It's not for pleasure. It is for the days when there was no electricity — you just swung gently on the swing and made the air move around you. A fallacy, like we think the sun is moving around us, whereas we are moving around the sun. Matters not, there is relative motion.

So, those of you who would not subject to extreme pain must understand that you cannot enjoy extreme pleasure, too — in no field of human existence. Then we are at the midpoint — as I repeat, gentle swings. No pleasure, no pain, no danger, no frustration, but a benign, calm, fulfilled existence. Then I begin to think of my Self. My problems in existence are over. I know now I have a Self inside. I seek someone who can tell me what it is. He says, "Sit and meditate. I cannot tell you what it is. You have to perceive it, experience it in yourself." Through this meditation I become aware that there is something in me which is not the **me** I thought I was. I begin to go more and more towards it. As I go more and more towards the east, I am inevitably going more and more away from the west. No need to renounce. By the fact of turning inwards, I am turning away from the external. Automatically, the renunciation that people have tried for centuries to achieve and failed, is in my hands, is in my grasp. I renounce without renouncing, because I am walking towards the right thing, the right goal — my inner Self. Why do I have to be ascetic? Why do I have to renounce? Why do I have to give away — "Take up thy bed and walk" — why the bed? "Sell all thou hast and follow me." Why sell all thou hast? Why not come with all thou hast, too? Did not Jesus even, require two loaves and five fishes to feed the multitude? He could not feed from nothing. Why two loaves and five fishes? Why not one loaf and one fish? Why not zero loaves and zero fish? It is a proof that no miracle can be created or performed without some material base to it. It is not possible. I can make a tree from a seed, but I cannot create a tree from nothing. One seed — yes, it is possible. But every seed? Will it give a tree? We don't know, because we are dealing with living beings, living things which are not subject to the law of transmutation, like metals.

In the material world, you knock off one electron from an atom — you have changed it. Knock off a second electron — you have changed it again. Add a third electron — it has come back to what it was in between. Add many electrons and many orbits — it has become something else. It is easy. But if tomorrow the moon is knocked off, will the earth change? If the children in a family are knocked off one by one, does the man change? He may, he may not. He may change in the right direction, he may change in the wrong direction. He may think of it as a merciful act in which God took away his children and said, "They have been blessed. I am left here to suffer." Or he may curse God and say, "You bloody so and so, you know, S.O.B. You are cruel beyond measure. You have taken away my child." And God laughs and says, "Your child? Damn fool! A moment of pleasure in bed and you think it is your child? What did you do for it? Did you want it? Did you create it? Were you not miserable when it was born? One more mouth to feed! And now you say, 'It is my child you have taken away.' When was it yours?"

So if my child is not mine, if my wife is not mine — after all, she came to me as an alliance, as we say in India. Alliances are always being broken, today more than ever before. Political alliances, matrimonial alliances, everything, you see. There is even the case of a boy of twelve or so divorcing his parents in America — it made history. So today we are living in times where alliances are being broken. I believe there is a purpose behind this. Alliances are being broken to enable us to forge a new alliance which will be eternal. And to be eternal, that alliance must only be forged with one who is eternal. I cannot have a friend for eternity, because tomorrow he may die, tomorrow I may be dead. What is this eternity of friendship? Foolish Greeks, foolish Plato with his Lysis! What is friendship? It is a meeting of two passengers in a train, friends from the time they come together to the time one gets off the train. It may last for one station, it may last for a few days. No more. Husband and wife? Same. Father and children, mother and children? Same. All temporal, impermanent bonds. Therefore the Gita says, "*anityam asukham lokam.*" This world is impermanent, and can give only unhappiness.

"*Anityam asukham lokam,*" and the *Gitacharya* asks, "How do you expect to find anything but pain in this world, intemperance in this world, impermanence in this world?" Look for it elsewhere. My kingdom is not of this world. That kingdom of transcendent love, transcendent benignity, transcendent eternality is somewhere else — it is in my Self. The tragedy is, we cannot separate myself into its two components — me and my Self. I am not my Self. So the *Upani-*

shad says, "That by which the eye sees, that by which the ear hears," because the ear by itself doesn't hear anything. When it is dead, all the turmoil and clamour of this world does not penetrate. All the *agarbatthis* you put around a corpse to prevent its stink from coming out has no effect on the corpse. All the beautiful women weeping around it have no effect. If they had wept for him in his life, he might have achieved something, but they only tempted him, led him into misery, led him into the mire of despond, sloughs of despond, and now they are weeping. What is the use of a beautiful woman weeping by the corpse, when she should have wept during his lifetime and said, "Damn fool, get away! Escape while it is still possible. Let not your senses drag you hither and thither, where we are." So you see, death is of no use to such a person. The people around him are of no use. The *sugandh* around him is of no use. The prayers around him are of no use. Nothing is of any use, unless he had the wisdom to convert **this** into the absolutely eternally convertible thing which we must do in our lifetime. It is not possible after death.

Many people asked Babuji, "Can we progress after we are dead?" If you are liberated, yes. Therefore, liberation is the **minimum** that we have to achieve in this life — the absolute minimum. It is no progress, it is just escape. Then some sort of progress through eternity becomes possible, unimpeded by grossness, because the soul has no grossness. So if you are not willing to do anything else, at least make sure of your liberation, because without liberation you are back again, into another body, into another *harem*, into another sensory world, into another arena of temptation, danger, fear, despond. So an awareness of the self, the existence of something inside me which is making me, myself, exist, is an absolute requirement — the bottom line for a spiritual search

Love Thy Neighbour As Thyself

to begin. It is no use coming here as businessmen, as beautiful women, you know, as wise people to find out.

Therefore, something which is very commonly misunderstood in Sahaj Marg — that we begin at the sixth step of yoga. Why? One, two, three, four, five — they don't bother us. Six, seven, and eight — they apply to us, because through *dhyana*, *dharana* becomes possible, *samadhi* becomes possible. The other five steps we are supposed to have already created for ourselves by right living **before** we come to the Guru. *Asana* is only sitting in a right pose for the duration of the meditation. We are supposed to have created that ability, not lounge around like these pampered Americans, you know, and Europeans. They are not comfortable anywhere. Give them six cushions, they want a seventh. Give them seven, they want a ninth. Put them in an air-conditioned room, they must have the temperature exact, and you know, they are fiddling around with the thermostat. Put them in a soundproof room, yet the dog barking next door seems to penetrate to their ears, and they want the dog in the next house chained up and put away. How will they ever meditate?

The senses — they have indulged so much — those damned senses have become a damnation for them. Their ears are too sensitive — a neighbour's radio at night somewhere, three furlongs away is a nuisance for them, and this absolutely stupid fairy tale of the princess sleeping on seven mattresses over a pea, and she could not sleep all night, which is held up as the acme of sensitivity, is a curse on the Western race. We sleep on stones! It's a common sight in India to see a man sleeping on a lorry or a truck laden with rubble, you know, going for construction. And he is there sleeping, *insha allah,* happily. The jolting truck, because we don't have fine roads, yet the man feels nothing though every piece of rock has so many points, and the glaring sun striking down at him — and he is happy he is asleep!

The Westerners, with all their intellectual arrogance, their material wealth, their affluence, their comforts — the first day in India, and I have to pray for them! "Lord, let them go back home alive!" This is my prayer, you see, because which one of them will collapse under the stress and strain of the Indian condition, nobody knows. For us, it is our everyday life. I warn you Gujaratis here — don't become so affluent or so addicted to comfort that when you come to India you suffer, and you cannot meditate. You have to run to the toilet, every fly and mosquito becomes a menace to your meditation. In India, above all lands on this Earth, the conditions are absolutely perfect to make you a meditater *par excellence*. People in Europe don't know how to meditate, and if they are able to meditate in Europe, they cannot meditate in India. And one who cannot meditate in India is not meditating.

So, make sure that you have European minds, but Indian hearts. One requirement above all, that Babuji said was the most essential — to have an Indian heart and a European mind. The perfect combination for a yogi. Not a recluse who ran away from society out of selfish self-interest for his own self-evolution, but a thinking being. You know, *homo sapiens sapiens*, not *homo sapiens*, as many people foolishly say. *Homo sapiens sapiens*. We are *homo sapiens sapiens*. We are thinking beings capable of thinking about thinking, and we have to think of others.

Every rich man knows that if he is in the middle of Soweto in his palace, he may not wake up tomorrow morning. Why? Because he is surrounded by misery, by pain, by

Love Thy Neighbour As Thyself

poverty, by need. How can he, alone, be prosperous in that community? So to be safe, to be secure, you must convert the society in which you are living. Like a stone which is dropped in the centre of a pond — I think in a sense it retains its place there by sending out ripples of its presence, to the ends of eternity if it is possible. Such waves don't die down. And we? We are sitting here thinking we are rich, we are wise, and nothing is coming out of us to change even the innermost circles of our society. Our friends are still foolish businessmen. Our wives are still pretty dolls. Our children are still drug addicts. How is it possible that a mere stone dropped in a pond can create ripples through the entire expanse of that pond or lake? And we being what we are, create no ripples even within our own family circle. Are we not even as heavy as a stone? Unfortunately, I have to say yes. Even the stone has more effect than you.

What are you, you useless beings, who cannot create a ripple in society in which you are existing? On the contrary, you allow the lake to smother out the waves! How is it possible? Instead of a tiny pebble creating waves in the lake, the lake is killing the waves, and we say, "My society, my *biradari*, my brotherhood, my Gujarati community, my *patidar* — what will I do? They will ostracize me. I will not be accepted in society. My daughter will not be married. My son will not get a place in school." Try it! After all, it was a Gujarati, a simple, foolish Gujarati who changed the politics of India, who gave it its freedom — a mere Mohandas Karamchand Gandhi. Not a saint by any means, but he **achieved**. Why? Because he was not afraid of his community, he was not afraid of his society, he was not afraid of his caste.

Heart of the Lion

He was a *baniya* (merchant), and you know, in India when you say he is a *baniya*, there is a stink behind that word. It is not used as a word of praise. It is used as a word of opprobrium, criticism. "*Baniya sala!*" That's what we say. The *sala* is inevitable. But he was a *baniya* too, Mohandas Karamchand Gandhi. What set him apart from all the other *baniyas*? You see, there is another *baniya* — I don't know whether he is really a *baniya* — who has started teaching about urine therapy, who was ridiculed, poor fellow. There was another *baniya* who drank goat's milk and five or six peanuts, and he became very much something like a saint, though he was never a saint. He was a great man, but not all great men are saints, and very few saints have ever become great men. So greatness and saintliness don't go together. It's only the politically saintly people who have become great — Aurobindo, Gandhi. Some spirituality with a great deal of public acclaim, political activity, political, shall we say successes, that made them great. Aurobindo would not have become great but for his revolutionary activities.

What happened to Ramakrishna? You don't find Ramakrishna Streets, you only find Vivekananda Road, Vivekananda Avenues. What happened to the man who made Vivekananda? He is forgotten. Which is a secret you see, that the father must subdue and subordinate himself to his son's greatness. That is the way of progress — each generation greater than the previous one, not in the sense of the previous one having been less, but the present one being great. Not that I love Caesar less, but that I love Rome more. It's not I love myself less, but that I love my Self more. Not that I love materiality less, but that I love spirituality more.

Sahaj Marg does not preach an ascetic way of life. It preaches a family way of life, a sensible family way of life. A

Love Thy Neighbour As Thyself

loving family, a harmonious family, all contributing to the joint progress of all. Not a poor husband and a rich wife fulminating against him and saying, "You damn fool from Nadiad! How did I marry you? *Gawar, dehati.*" Or a rich man marrying a poor girl, and saying she doesn't even know how to make tea — forget *dokla.* "*Chai nahin bana sakti to dokla kahan se banayegi!*"

But a balanced family, where two things come together, mutually elevating each other, loving each other, in harmony with each other, knowing that if the family is not complete in every respect, that individual has created no ripples, the family cannot create any ripples. If the family cannot create ripples, that society cannot create ripples. Therefore we are living in a ripple-less society, everybody afraid of rocking the boat lest we create ripples. "*Nahi nahi, rahne do, tikh hein, chaal se!*" *Chaal se?* What *chaal se?*

The only thing which goes on eternally without any help from us is the Devil. God needs our help to help us. And what is this help that we have to give Him? Babuji called it co-operation. Co-operation — to work together with. God can lift a mountain. God can revolve a planet. He can twist the universe around into nothing. But he cannot change a human being, because what changes a human being is not God — it is himself. And God says, "But my son — here too, I help you. Everything else in nature I do from outside, but to help you I have come inside you. I am residing in your heart as your Self, but you have ignored me through eternity. I am something which cannot be shifted and moved around. I am there, as I am everywhere. I cannot help being there. Don't think I love you because I am inside you. It is inevitable, because He who is everywhere cannot avoid being in you, too. Don't take it as a sign of special recognition, and say,

'Aha! My Self is in me, therefore I am blessed.' Not at all. You are as cursed as the cursed criminal in jail. He, too, has me inside himself. What is the difference between you and him? You a multimillionaire, he a poor murderer in jail — both of you have me inside you. What is the difference? So, don't crow about the Self in you until you see me inside you, hand yourself over to me so that now, instead of you, I am there. Then you become different from the criminal in the jail. Then, having me inside you, and knowing that I am you, and nothing else, you become capable of helping others."

Who can help others? All this trash, you know, social service — we cannot really touch even the surface of this. Why? Because we are working from outside. It's like painting a decaying wall — cosmetic. The wall is going, and frantically every year I am painting it so that the decay may not show.

Even corpses are dressed up. They are shaved, they are rouged, they are dressed up in suits and put in coffins to be presentable before burial. Presentable to whom, for heaven's sake? What we would not do for a man in life, we are willing to do for him in death. Why? Because for once and for all we are rid of that fellow. "Goodbye. If during life, if I had to spend on you like this, I would have had to give you thirty suits and a shave every day. Now, one set of suits, and one shave, and one application of rouge on your cheeks — my duty to you is done." Therefore we honor the dead. *Uthavana* (obituary), we see in the Hindi press every day, and we see photographs of the parent, supposed to be put in by holy, loving children. "Seth Manikchand Hukumchand — gone but not forgotten. Forever in our hearts." Blah, blah. Lies!

So you see, the knowledge of the Self, the recognition that it is in me, the growth towards loving the Self that is in

Love Thy Neighbour As Thyself

me, loving it so much that I say, "Now you are my being." Every fool of a man is telling every fool of a girl, "You are my heart. You are my sweetheart!", when my real sweetheart is here. This heart must become sweet, because in it resides my Self — me as I am to become, me as I was when this creation began. The me which has adopted this set of attributes and a body so that it may come to this consciousness, this recognition of its ultimacy, of its eternality, so that it will burst out of its cocoon.

This transformation that we see in nature — a moth coming out of what we thought was a worm. Resplendent in its beauty, flying around where this ugly worm was lying, unable to move even. This transformation is not really a transformation. It is only the Self shedding all its outward prisons — the prison of the body, the prison of the senses, the prison of the mind — freeing itself in the ultimate freedom which we call liberation. And if it has gone about its purpose seriously, with conviction, with faith, with determination above all, at that moment of liberation it enters the eternity which was its source. This is spirituality.

Not what we are toying around with, not what we are playing with — pretending to meditate, coming for a sitting when we are miserable with some tears. When we are happy, looking at the wristwatch — "When is this fellow going to stop the sitting? It's already twenty-two minutes! For heaven's sake, what is this nonsense? Babuji has said three minutes is enough." So let us not play hide-and-seek with ourselves. We have hidden from the Self so long. We cannot afford to hide from the Self anymore. We don't have to seek, because it is there, where it has always been — in me. So why hide and seek? From whom can I hide? Whom shall I seek? When He whom I seek and he who seeks are but, in a sense, the same.

So I hope this wisdom will dawn upon all of you, and you will treat Sahaj Marg not merely as sitting in the morning, cleaning in the evening, prayer and meditation at night — blah, blah, blah, blah, blah, you see — like so much of whiskey and so much of soda, so much of tomato juice and so much of Worcestershire sauce. This is not a breakfast or a lunch or a dinner. It is not even pleasure in bed, that we should read a Kinsey book this size, to know what every damn fool of a human being has known. Only stupid fools should read Kinsey reports and pornographic novels and titillate themselves, to do what should be natural to every human being, male or female. Why is it necessary? Because that ingredient alone which makes even sex pleasurable is lacking. And what is it? Love. And what is this love that is lacking? That I must love the other as I love my Self. If I do that, sex becomes holy, becomes divine, becomes creative. Otherwise it is only an act of lustful breeding.

"Love thy neighbour as thyself" — a most potent statement. Not possible until I love my Self, because Christ says, "Love thy neighbour as thyself." He did not just say, "Love thy neighbour." It should have been enough! Love your friend, love your girlfriend, love your father. But as thyself? Are you able to do it? "No, my Lord. I am not able to do it." "Why?" "Because I don't love my Self." He who loves himself can love others. He who does not love himself cannot love anybody else, anything else. He hates everything. The small pebble which stubs his toe when he is out for a walk becomes a menace. He kicks it furiously and pains himself more. You know that classic example of a man who kicks

Love Thy Neighbour As Thyself

something which is in his path and then runs around on one foot, waiting for his wife to come and sympathize with him.

Learn to love thy Self — this is the first law of spirituality. Forget the neighbour, because if you are able to do this — why only the neighbour? The man in the next city, the man in the next country, the man in the next planet, the man in the next galaxy, we will love. Then universal love becomes possible, because I am loving that in me which is universal. Through that universal love for the universal, universal love becomes possible outside myself, too. Not an individual, incremental love of one plus one plus one — but at one stroke, I love Him who loves all, He is in me, therefore I become capable of universal love. Thank you.

The Beauty of the Heart
April 23, 1993

Some preceptors have been asking me how to be successful in their work. In spirituality, the word *success* doesn't feature at all. It's not in our dictionary. So where there is no success, there is no failure also, because success and failure are opposites. In spirituality we deal neither with success nor with failure. The work of the preceptor, the work of the Master, never fails.

I am reminded of a story about a young boy who was going back from school to his house, and he saw an old man of sixty-five or seventy planting a mango seed. And he stopped and said, "Grandfather, grandfather, you are planting this mango, but do you think you will live to eat its fruit?" He said, "My grandson, I may not, but somebody will eat of the fruit of this tree." It is only the selfish who plant seeds hoping to eat the fruit of that plant himself, or herself. Nature does not plant for us. Nature plants, and whoever is there at the right time, in the right place, benefits. That is why Babuji Maharaj said, "Such a time may not come again for the next so-many thousands of years, when spirituality shall be available so easily." This is the time. This is the place.

There was a story I once read, you see, about a lady who was going shopping and sees a new shop. She walks in, she is amazed because she knows all the shops in the neighbourhood, but there's a new one. She walks in, and there she sees God standing behind the counter. And God asks her, "Yes, my daughter, what do you want?" She says, "God, I want beauty, I want health, I want happiness, not only for myself but for all mankind." God smiles compassionately and says, "My dear, I don't sell these things. I only give you seeds. You have to cultivate the rest."

So you see, even God does not give us these things ready-made. Therefore it is foolish to pray to God for these things. We have to sow the seed, nurture it, water it until it germinates, then protect it as much as we can, not expecting anything in return. This is very important. Because, you know, suppose you have a packet of one hundred seeds, and you look at them and select what you think are the ten best and you plant them. Nothing may come out of that, because we don't know which seed is the best seed. Because the true life of the seed is inside.

I told you the story of Yagnavalkya and his disciple this morning — when, under the Master's instructions the disciple cut open the seed, there was nothing there. Now, how are we to know what is the value of this 'nothing' in the seed which makes it into a giant *ficus*? We do not have the capacity to judge from a state of nothingness what the something is going to be, which will be manifested out of that state of nothingness.

Therefore we have all these stories in our *Puranas* in the ancient Hindu tradition, for instance, of different people creating different things out of nothingness. A magician brings something from under the handkerchief. Another magician brings a chicken and seventeen eggs from out of an empty top hat. Lord Krishna, from the *akshayapatra* feeds multitudes. Christ, with two loaves and five fishes — not really nothing, but something, you know, like seeds.

The Beauty of the Heart

So you see, human capacity is not in failure or success. Human capacity must be manifested in being active. The Gita says, "*Karmanye vaadikaaraste maa phaleshu kadhaachana.*" "You have a right to do your duty, not to expect the fruits thereof." The fruits are mine, the Lord says. Of course, those who are inclined to be Communist will say, "What is this? This is another form of capitalism! I work, and he takes the result. It's the black man's and the white man's situation all over again. Here the devotee is the black man, God is the white man, you see, waiting to cut off the fruits and harvest it for himself." Not so. We are not now talking about factories where we deal with inanimate matter which we can melt, which we can mold, which we can turn, which we can cut up into pieces, re-mold. How automobiles are made, planes are made, implements are made, tools are made. We are not creating tools here.

In spirituality, as in agriculture, we are dealing with living things, and nobody can predict what will happen to a living thing, because the living thing has a will of its own, has a samskara of its own. As they say, combining two proverbs, "You can train a dog, but you cannot straighten its tail!" You may put the tail into a straight tube and tie it up for twenty years, but open it and it will spring back into its original curved shape. But the dog can be trained. So here, who are we supposed to train? The dog is obedient. We tempt it, we terrify it — two instruments of religion, as Babuji Maharaj always said — fear and temptation. Keep a rolled-up newspaper to hit it on its snout when it misbehaves, and a biscuit to feed it when it behaves well. But human beings don't react even to fear and temptation. That is why there is so much of AIDS today. No fear of AIDS, therefore AIDS. It almost seems as if that which you are not afraid of will surely assail you, like a man going to the jungle in bravado, saying,

"I don't need a gun or a knife. I am not afraid of lions," and just behind him, hears, "Grrrrrr!" It doesn't come from in front, it comes from behind.

It is said in the Upanishad, for instance, that of the *Panchabhutas* it is said, "*Mrityurdhaavati panchama iti.*" Death is chasing all these five things, the five senses. It is always behind. Then there is another story of a woodcutter, who was cutting wood for his living every day and bringing a head-load home every evening, selling part of it, using part of it, going on for years like this. And one day in the jungle he is tying up his bundle of firewood to take home — he feels afraid. For no reason, he feels a strange presence, you see, and he starts walking fast. And pit-pat, pit-pat, pit-pat, the footsteps are following behind. He runs. The footsteps run behind him. Finally, you know, he makes a terrific effort, trying to run away from this thing which is following him, and falls exhausted, and then he sees — God. He says, "What is this? I have been looking for you all my life. Where have you been?" He says, "My son, it was always me who was trying to catch you, trying to follow you and catch you, but you have been eternally running away from me. Today you are caught!"

So you see, on one side we have this idea of death, who is pursuing us inexorably with his loop in his hand, like the lasso of, you know, the Western cowboy. In the Hindu tradition, it is the lasso which is thrown around — it is called the *yama-paasha*, and it works in such a way that the soul is removed from the body. The body falls, and the soul goes away with the Yama-dhoota or Yama himself. Simultaneously, God is also following.

Now, whom should we think is following us? Who is it who is following me all my life? If I am afraid, I think it is death. If I am a devotee, I think it is my Master. Master always said, "Think the Master is behind you in everything that you are doing. On the stray occasions when you are afraid — for instance, when you are going to a new place in the darkness — think the Master is going in front of you." So, fear puts the Master in front. Devotion put Him just behind. In both cases he must be with us — in fear, during temptation, in confidence. Without the Master we are nothing. Either He must be in front of me, or He must be behind me. Preferably He should be all around me, surrounding me like the praetorian guard around the emperor.

So, what is the need for fear? What do we need to be tempted by? We should be tempted by Him, go towards Him, where temptation works as love for us, not as something, you know, teasing us towards His presence, like we tease children towards ourselves, or birds towards ourselves. We should be afraid that we do not displease Him. Fear has its function, too. As Babuji said, "*Kama* and *krodha* are divine attributes, given to us by Divinity itself." *Kama* — love for Him. This is what in the *puja paddati*, you see, in temples when you offer *prasad* and they put on this *dhoop*, for instance, or the lamp, and they wave it around the idol and then they bless you, "*Ishta kaamyartha phalasiddhyartham.*" It does not mean "what you desire." It means, "He who you should desire. Let Him bless you with His presence." That is God. But we think, you know — the childless woman thinks it is her child that will be given. The loveless wife thinks her husband will suddenly start loving her. The moneyless beggar thinks he will get money. *Kama* has come to mean all these low things — desire, titillation, lust, food — you know, when we eat like pigs, gluttony — miserliness. The priest said, "*Ishta kaamyartha phalasiddhyartham.*" "I will get what I want. I will get what I desire." *Kama* has come to mean **desire**. But *kama*, in its original purity, in its high meaning, meant **love**.

So you see, God can only give us love, because He is only love. Like a honey can only give us sweetness — you cannot expect salt taste out of honey. You cannot expect a cucumber to taste like a pizza. Isn't it? You should not expect a human being to behave like an animal. Why do we behave like animals, like birds and beasts of the air — destructive, with talons and teeth? Because of our samskaras. Things are still left in us from our ancient fall into the lowest levels, when we started our original descent from there, and we are still trying to work them away. But we cannot work it away by a conscious act of renunciation — "I will no longer behave like a bullock," for instance. "I will not try to gore everybody I meet." It doesn't work, because the samskara inside is stronger than me.

So I have to submit to somebody, you see, who can tame me. Babuji used to be very pleased when Dr. Varadachari used to say of himself, that he was the tamed animal of God. This is the old symbol of the *vaahana*, you see — the vehicle of the Lord. Somebody flying on a peacock, somebody on a garuda, somebody mounting the buffalo, Ganesh on his small *chuchundar*. The idea was that each of these gods, in the pantheon of the Hindu gods, he is responsible for elevating that particular life form by his own efforts, by taming it.

It is like we have dog trainers, lion trainers, pigeon trainers. Unfortunately we have no human trainers. I have always felt that the human being needs more training than a dog! A dog is easily trained. Human beings are not amenable to discipline. The more you try to train them, the more they run away or resist. Therefore the training has to be subtle. Even parents would be well advised to try subtlety on their chil-

The Beauty of the Heart

dren, not authority. "I say so! I am your father. Come on, do it!" One day, he is your height, and he says, "Come, Dad. Can it! What were you when you were my age? Grandma told me, you see, how you used to be a rambunctious blighter! Stealing the butter, hitting the dog, throwing stones at the neighbours, stealing apples from the opposite garden. You are no better than I am." And the father has nothing to say, you see, because he was all these things. The trouble is, when we are accused of something, all the goodness in us, the positive things in us, fall back. We cannot also say, "No, no, my son. I was also the man who gave the beggar ten paise" And the child says, "Big deal! Ten paise out to the beggar. Big deal, Daddy, and how much have you in your bank?" He says, "You know all that?" He says, "Yes, Mummy showed me your passbook. It runs into seven figures. Ten paise out to the beggar — big deal!"

So you see, we are voiceless before our children. Really, today's children are not susceptible, are not amenable to what they call blackmail in any form. Modern children talk of blackmail all the time. When mummy is very loving, they say, "Oh, this blackmail of love, Chariji — I don't like it. Look at my mummy smirking from there." I said, "But why do you think like that?" She said, "Yes, but Chariji, they are always trying the blackmail on me. If it is not the blackmail of sweets or pocket money, it is this business of love — 'Don't you love me, darling? Don't you love me enough to do this for me?'" Children are not fools. Adults are fools, children are very wise.

That is why the Hindu pantheon of *rishis* is so full of *rishis* who became *rishis* before they were in their teens. They didn't wait to be forty-five, and fifty, and sixty — gray haired, bearded, toothless idiots. That is why in the

Heart of the Lion

Brahmanic tradition the child must have its *upanayana*, what we call, you know, this *yagnopavitam*, before it is eight years, counting from its day of conception, which is the seventh year of terrestrial life. Catch 'em young! If at that time, when they are amenable to discipline, when they are idealistic, when they want to be everything that is good and nice and great and beautiful in this world, if at that time we could give them the proper guidance, we would produce a race of angels.

Unfortunately in today's life, the children are corrupted from the very beginning. "You must be like daddy." For heaven's sake, which daddy? Is there a daddy here among us who is worth emulating by the children? Forgive me for asking this question, but I ask it in a sincere spirit. How many of us can answer, "Yes," and say, "Yes, I really wish my child to be like me." How many women are there here who can say, "Yes, I want my daughter to be like me." In what sense? Lipstick? Powder? Silk saris? That is easy to emulate. You give a beggar woman five hundred rupees, she will emulate you in no time at all. Which parent here, male or female, will have the guts to stand up and say, "Yes, I am such a one, whom I would love my child to be like." They don't exist. So what do you mean by saying, "You must be like Daddy," or "You must be like Mummy"? And the child says, "For heaven's sake, Mum. Not that crap again! I don't want to be like Daddy." "Yes, but he's a successful lawyer." "But Mummy, you know what people say about him." "Yes, but you know, today you cannot be an honest lawyer, son." "Yes, but then I don't want to be a lawyer." "But Daddy has such an immense practice. He wants somebody to help him. Do you want this money to go out of the family?" The age-old argument, you see, by which we capture our daughters-in-law, by which we capture our daughters, put them in this

The Beauty of the Heart

meshed golden parrot's cage, because money should not go out of the family — Patel marrying Patel, Patidar marrying Patidar, Islam marrying Islam, Christian marrying Christian — what is this rubbish?

What were Adam and Eve? Buddhists? Christians? Hindus? Can you answer that question, Charlie? What is God? Is He a Hindu or a Muslim? You know, in Madurai we have this famous temple of Meenakshi. She is a *vaishnavite*, because she is Lord Vishnu's sister, and she marries Shiva. It is supposed to be the first *shaivite-vaishnavite* marriage. It is like the marriages in politics, you see, where Akbar married many Hindu wives, trying to reconcile the Hindus and the Muslims. Doesn't work, because you are still conscious that you are marrying a Muslim wife, and the Muslim girl is still conscious that she is marrying a Hindu. So she remains a Muslim in her heart, while he remains a Hindu, and now they fight in bed and out of it, all the time, remaining one the Muslim and one the Hindu. She goes to mosque, he goes to a *mandir*. There is no unification because that which divided you originally, your religion, is still there. It has not been thrown aside and said, "No. I am a human being marrying another human being, full of love." We continue to be German wife, Swedish husband. Chinese husband, Japanese wife. Australian Aboriginal wife with a Timbuktu man. And we are ever-conscious, you see, and we also feel pride, as if we have humbled ourselves in marrying this wonderful beauty from, I don't know, Zululand, and we go around saying, "Oh, I married a black woman, you know. It's wonderful. You should try it!" If you are still conscious that she is black and you are white, damn you and your marriage. If you are still conscious that there is a God and there is a you, damn you and your spirituality.

Heart of the Lion

That is the secret behind constant remembrance — no more difference between Him about whom I think all the time, and myself. Because in the ancient tradition of Sahaj Marg, I am what I think I am. If I think I am a fool, I am a fool. If I am afraid and I think I am afraid, I am afraid. "What is there to be afraid of?" "I don't know." "All right, go and see a psychiatrist." "What is it you are afraid of?" "Everything." "Oh. Bad case. I can treat somebody who is afraid of something, or some things. But everything?" "Yes, but Chariji, I am afraid of the day." "Are you happy at night?" "No, no, I am worse at night!" "Then when are you really unafraid?" "Sometimes when I sit in meditation, but then too, you know, I close my eyes and when I see the darkness inside I am not able to meditate anymore." Now, what can you do with such people?

Christianity says, "Perfect love casteth out fear." Love and fear cannot exist simultaneously. One who says he loves his master cannot be afraid of that master. If he is afraid he does not love. "No, no, I did not mean afraid in that sense, Chariji, but you know, there is always some fear. What to say? I don't know of any other word." Wonderful — learn English better. "I am nervous of the Master." Why? Then you don't love. You have only affection for the Master.

So you see, we are too much hypocritical in our approach to spirituality, to the Master, to ourselves. "I am a good man, Chariji. Why do I need spirituality?" Sometimes I feel like, you know, Christ taking up a stone and saying, "Should I beat you if you have no sins?" Who is the good man today? Who is the good woman today? Just because you go to the temple and donate twenty thousand rupees or rands to the Patidar hall, and put your name on some subscription lists for the blind, for the poor, for the lame, for the blacks.

The Beauty of the Heart

Does it qualify you to be called a good man or a good woman?

Just because you invite a few rich guests and feed them opulently doesn't mean you are good. You are only showing off. You are only blatantly throwing your riches in other people's faces. "Look at me, I can afford five sweets for dinner." Wonderful. Will you also give your guests money to treat themselves with next day when they fall sick? Ideally, such guests, such hosts should give them all envelopes containing, you know, at least a hundred rand each, and say, "You know, all this opulence I have hypocritized you with today — you are going to fall sick tomorrow. This will be Dr. Mukund's consultation fee. Keep it. You will need it, because I have been showing off. There is no love behind these sweets. I just want to show off, you see. My house is a show off, my *puja* room is for showing off. My wife, even, is on display — well-rouged, well-lipsticked, well-coiffed."

Many of these wives go to what they call these, you know, beauty clinics. When they have a big dinner — let us say like somebody like Kasturbhai Lalbhai is coming to dinner. First thing she does is not cook — that, the cook does. She goes to the beauty clinic, pays three hundred fifty rupees or seven hundred rupees, and comes back looking awful! (laughter) And then she is so sanctimonious about her good looks, the husband wants to kiss her, you know, behind the refrigerator door, for instance, and she says, "No!" The first seed of dissension is when women pretend to be beautiful and dress themselves up. This man says, "Yes, but what the hell are you looking good for? What are you looking beautiful for? For whom are you looking beautiful, if not for the husband? Is it for someone else?" They have no answer. That night they are both lying awake, both in anger, and if they are not quickly going to make up, that will go into days and weeks of anger, and probably a separation.

Beauty is not conducive to well-being. Women should like to be simple — naturally beautiful with such beauty as they have got. "*Bhaarya roopavati shatru*" says the Sanskrit proverb. "A beautiful wife is a man's enemy." "*Bhaarya roopavati shatru.*" Why? Because she is eternally tempting him to do things which he should not be doing. I mean, there is a limit to even what we call marital happiness. But when she goes around looking like, what do you call them, these models, this fellow, all his lusts are stirred up, you see, and he says, "Come," and she says, "No. Not today, not again, for heaven's sake!" Now what will that poor man do? Bad enough having beautiful faces to pass on the streets without stopping your car. It's worse at home because she's always there. "Damn it!", he says. "What can I do?" "*Bhaarya roopavati shatru.*" All women should learn this and put it up on their, you know, bathroom mirrors. "*Bhaarya roopavati shatru.*" — look at it every morning.

We see this in the ancient tradition, how *rishi patnis* were tempted. Even the great *rishi patnis* were tempted. Goddesses have been tempted. Gods have been tempted. Indra has been tempted again and again. You go to the Greek tradition, the Roman tradition — Jove seems to be doing nothing but looking down at the Earth to see which beauty he can next pick up from there, you see, and take to Heaven. The Greek tradition is full of this — lust, lust, lust. No love — love is reserved for homosexuality — platonic love, they call it. You see what a corrupt tradition, philosophically, historically, esthetically, in literature we have inherited from the past, whether it is the Hindu tradition or the Greek tradition or the Roman tradition.

The Beauty of the Heart

Now we have to undo all this nonsense. Put beauty where it belongs — in the heart. Beauty is not of the face. There is a Jagjit Singh *gazal*, you know. He says, "One expects a beautiful person to have a hard heart. But why do you, my dear?", he asks his ugly beloved. "Why do you have a hard heart?" Beauty and hard heart go together. For the men, wealth and hard heart go together. Therefore, in philosophy, in spirituality, these two things are always frowned upon. Don't think I am being partial to the men — what is a curse for women, namely their beauty, the curse for man is his wealth. Such people find it very difficult to even enter spirituality. Because the woman is too busy preening herself, you know. A really beautiful woman takes about two hours to make up her hair, another hour to make up her face. The lipstick takes very long, and of course the *sari*, you know, what a simple woman can wear in about thirty seconds, it takes them three hours. So when are they going to meditate? And the rich man is perpetually jumping between his office and his bank, either taking loans or giving loans.

So, there is an ancient wisdom which says, "Do not be like a frog, jumping hither and thither." Look to the real beauty inside — the beauty of Him who is sitting there — the Self in you. Eternally resplendent, eternally illuminating everything it sees and it touches — it is **itself** resplendent. "*Koti surya samaprabha*," it is said in the *Puranas*. His brilliance is like the illumination of one crore suns. "*Koti surya samaprabha.*" Do you want that, or do you want the beauty of, I don't know, some Pond's cold cream and I don't know what else, you see — Revlon lipstick. We should not indulge in the beauty which can be wiped away by a sheet of paper.

I remember once, Babuji was kissed by a woman. You know, he was not aware of it — suddenly a woman darted and planted a kiss on his cheek, and he looked at my wife and said, "*Bahu, lipstick to nahin lag gaya yahan?*" Even he knew about lipstick, you see, living in Shahjahanpur. "*Lipstick nahin lag gaya?*" And then my wife said, "No, no, there is nothing. Don't worry." And then he said in Hindi, "This has happened in Europe. Okay. This is a depraved land, a fallen land, but suppose one of these European women come and plant a kiss on my cheek in my house when my granddaughters are there. What will they think?"

So whenever he found a woman even coming, you know, innocently to ask him a question, he would back off, like that — I'm not joking — literally he used to back off. And once he made a joke, you know, he said, "Next time, Parthasarathi, somebody comes to kiss me, I will send her to you!" I said, "Don't, because it will have to prolong your life on earth, because if I fall you will have to stay behind!" Then he became serious and said, "Nay, nay, I was only joking!"

So we should not dress up and make up in such a way that the guru is afraid. You understand? Therefore we are advised to go to temples not in rags, like in some traditions, but in a meek, simple way, like a woman who has been freshly washed — nothing on her face — no grease, no paint, no lipstick. We must go to God naked, it is said. Now, you know the value of nakedness, those of you who know the *Mahabharat* story. When Duryodan's mother asked him to come naked. She says, "I cannot bless you, but I can strengthen you. Come before me as you were born." That wily fellow Krishna on the way stops it, you see, and he puts something around his waist, and she opens her eyes for the first time in her life, and the whole of his body becomes like *vajra*, you know *vajra sharira*, but not the part he has covered up with a thin *dhoti*. And she says, "Why have you done

The Beauty of the Heart

this? You have not even obeyed me on the one occasion when I have given you an instruction." And he is lost. She berates him. She says, "How can you be naked before me? I bore you, and you think now you are a man? What is this foolishness?"

So you see, no covering — nakedness does not mean immediately taking off everything and coming before the Master like that. It means, "In all humility, I have nothing to hide. Not my outer self, not my inner self. I am pure. I don't need makeup. I am beautiful with an inner beauty which does not need embellishment. I am beautiful with an inner beauty which does not need the support of beauticians. My beauty is eternal. It does not fade with age. I am that which you want me to be. Now, my Lord, what do you want me to do?" He says, "Come." Babuji Maharaj used to say, "For such a one, the Master waits, perhaps eternally."

So, women should cultivate the beauty of the heart. The men, also, the beauty of the heart, because it is the heart which is doing us irreparable damage by being hard, by being cold, by being ungiving, but only demanding more and more. "Chariji, my heart says, you know, that my husband should love me better." People come to me in Europe with this sort of stupid statement. "Yes, but," I say, "Go and talk to your husband about it. Why do you come to me?" "No, no, if you pray, maybe he will love me more." Then I ask them the crucial question, "How much do **you** love your husband?" You see, even when there is an echo, I must sound something before the echo will come back to me. Everything originates in me. I must give before I can receive. Give and take.

I always make a joke with these Hindi-speaking people of North India, you see — "*Lena dena*" they say, whether it is Gujarat or North India. No "*Lena dena*" — "*Dena lena*."

Heart of the Lion

One who gives, receives. One who is only receiving will have to, by God, give. Otherwise he will die and be born again a hundred times before that debt is fulfilled. Why do you think great men are only giving — giving everything, giving themselves, giving their love, giving their life? Because in one grand, ultimate sacrifice you die for what you are working, and all the debts of your, I don't know, millions of past lives are repaid in that one grand, final sacrifice. Therefore you have this tradition of saints always being persecuted, tormented, tortured, crucified, or burned at the stake or buried alive — things like that.

One who must be, and wants to be, at the pinnacle of human perfection has to pay the price for it, and the price is your life. It cannot be otherwise. It is not just the removal of some petty samskaras, you see, some petty lusts. I am always remembering that story, you know, when a man came and was weeping and said, "I am a sinner. Please save me." And he was asked, "What sin have you committed that you think you are so great a sinner?" He said, "No, no, I have sinned." He said, "What sin? A bottle of wine? A woman? Which fool has not done these things? Come back to me when you have done something original!" Can any of you think of any original sin here? It doesn't exist. From time immemorial, you see, we have been doing these things. There is nothing new about lust or drunkenness or avarice or greed. Don't think you are creating some new trails, blazing new trails in the sinful history of this world. You are not capable. Any fool can go astray. It doesn't take much more than foolishness to do it. Like any man driving a car can have an accident — a moment of inattention and he is dead. A moment of weakness and you are a sinner!

The Beauty of the Heart

But to be a saint, eternally watchful, eternally alert, eternally devoted, eternally wanting that which you are wanting with a wanting which is beyond all wanting on Earth — craving — sleepless craving, restless craving. If that is not there, then you are at the mercy of the elements, of society, of habits, everything. If that is there, it is itself a protection, because in this utter restlessness for the one with whom you must be united, everything else is forgotten. I mean, you cannot remember anything else in that restlessness.

So Babuji Maharaj always speaks of restlessness. He speaks of craving. He speaks of nakedness. Not of wanting and longing and all these foolish terms, which are enough for human lovers — there must be a torment in one's life. Without it we are just pretending. A lover who is happy to be at home at 5:00 p.m. in the evening is no lover. "Oh, but I thought you were in love with so-and-so. Are you not going out?" "No, no, it's okay. Not every evening!" This is intellectual love. Now he is theorizing that if he goes to meet his beloved every evening, she will think it's a weakness. But you are weak, because this is not the weakness which is the opposite of strength. It is the weakness of foolishness, that there is no longing in your heart, and to whom will that girl eventually go? To one who loves her.

There is an old story, you see, about three boys who loved the same girl. They had all divine qualities. One could see to the end of this universe, for instance. Another could walk seven hundred miles in one step, and the third could do something similarly miraculous. And one day this girl died. She was buried in a *kabristan*. An old man, a saint comes and says, "You know, hidden beyond the seven seas and the seven mountains and the seven dungeons, past the seven dragons there is this golden vessel in which there is a medicine which, if brought and put on the lips of this dead girl, will make her alive again." So the far-seer looks and says, "I have located it." The far walker says, "Come, climb on my shoulders. We will go." The third man says, "Leave me to my peace here. I am tortured by her death. I cannot leave." And he is literally lying on the *kabristan* weeping his heart out. Eventually these two boys go, locate the medicine, and quickly come back with it. They open the *kabristan* and put the medicine on the girl's lips. She wakes up. Now, whom is she going to marry? The far walker says, "Without me, that blighter could not have gone there and brought the medicine." The far-seer says, "If I did not locate it, where would you be walking? You would still be walking, looking for it." Then they decide to leave it to the girl. She says, "I will marry this boy who was weeping here." And they are astounded. They said, "Why? We made you alive." She said, "Yes. You gave me the medicine which brought me to life. You are like my father because you have given me life. This man, with all his love for me, went and brought the medicine for me. He behaved like my brother. He is my brother — I cannot marry him. This man is my lover, because he spent all the time weeping on my graveyard here. He is my husband." And she marries him.

So the fruit always goes to love — not to beauty, not wealth. Of course, nowadays people buy things. Women buy with their beauty. Men buy with their money. Therefore you find this funny situation of beautiful women always in cars. You don't see beautiful women walking the streets anymore. They are in the Cadillacs and the Mercedes bought by the wealth of the man. Ashamed of themselves, secretly unhappy, miserable, longing for someone else perhaps, in Nadiad. I don't know where else, in Gujarat, and then they grow into this hypocrisy of life — "I am happy. I am Nagar-

The Beauty of the Heart

bhai Lalbhai's daughter, granddaughter, daughter-in-law, what-have-you, you see, and I am very happy. I have a palace to live in, a fleet of seven cars with fourteen drivers, seventeen cooks, untold lakhs of rupees spent on cosmetics. What more can a woman want?" She is a living mummy — not the living dead of spirituality, but the living mummy of absolute, cold death — heartless death, bought death, commercial death. A human being sold like a pig, like a dog, like cows.

Nor do you want real love. I am sure every woman, if she had the courage, would stand up and say, "Yes, I want real love." And so would the men. They are not happy with these beautiful girls in golden cages who respond to their every desire out of a submission, out of slavery.

Now, there is a difference between the submission of slavery and the submission of devotion. A devotee is not a slave, though he submits. As Babuji Maharaj said, "In spirituality there is service without servitude." We serve, but we are nobody's servants. This must be clearly understood. A preceptor is not the servant of the abhyasi. The Master is nobody's servant. He is his Master's servant. Therefore the Master goes around doing his work in obedience to **his** Master's wishes. The preceptor does his work in obedience to his Master's wishes. We are nobody's servants, nobody's slaves. We are free, because it is love which makes us accept this work — love for the Master. Don't mistake it as love for humanity, because if we mistake it for humanity, our love for humanity, we will have to pay the price that Christ paid, according to my Master, by his crucifixion. He pleaded with God and said, "I love human beings. I want to serve them." "Then," God said, "Die for them." It is very easy to mistake. For a cowherd to mistake the cows for his own. It is very easy for a *mali* to think that the garden is his because he is tending them and watering them and cutting them and planting them. The garden belongs to the Master, not to the gardener. The cattle belong to the owner, not to the cowherd. The children belong to God, not to the parents.

When we are able to realise all this with our heart and accept this with our heart, the beginning of humility will come. "I own nothing. I possess nothing. It is all His. Being His, I must look after it as if I am an honest, sincere trustee." Not the modern-day trustee, who only pander to their own, you know, pride and arrogance and ego. "Being a trustee, I must administer this trust faithfully. I must cultivate this garden to perfection. I must look after His children to perfection. Not my perfection, but their perfection. With love." Then we will see a society, a world which is transformed, because right down the line, from God to the lowermost inhabitant of the nether world, there will be this love pervading through the *saptalokas*, the seven worlds of creation, and there will be an instant of transformation. In one instant, the whole thing will be transformed. Transformation doesn't need time. Transformation needs understanding that, "This I am. This I don't want to be anymore." And if you remember the story of Babuji Maharaj when he was going to brush his teeth, walking up to the well, which is only probably six feet away from his chair, and this terrible longing came over him to be like Lalaji Maharaj, and he thought in his mind, "Oh, Master, I want to be like you!" Lalaji's voice answered, "You are already like me, my son."

So transformation is not a process. It is an instant in time which brings about transformation. But when we play with this transformation it can take millions of years — nobody knows. Then we are subject to the processes of a natural evolution, from the lower animal, to the higher animal, to the

The Beauty of the Heart

lower human, to the higher human, and go on through the angels. Then we need an eternity of time. So, one who says, "I have no time," will need this eternity of time. Beware! For one who says, "That is all?", he is instantly that.

Remember the beautiful story of Narada who was going to Heaven to meet the Lord, and on the way he met a madman dancing under a tree. The madman said, "Lord, where are you going?" Narada said, "I am going to the Lord in Heaven." He said, "Please, find out how many lives more I have to lead before I get liberated." Narada said, "So shall it be, my son. I will come back and give you the answer." A few miles further on, he sees a rishi meditating under the tree, and the rishi says, "Narada, you are going to Heaven to meet the Lord. Please find out when I am going to be liberated." He says, "Okay." In course of time he returns. The rishi is first. He says, "When will I be liberated?" Narada says, "The Lord said, 'Two more lives'," and the rishi beats his breast and weeps and wails. "What a cruel God. What a cruel destiny. Two more lives! What is all my *tapasya* worth?" And he is grovelling in the dust in despair, in misery. Narada smiles and walks on. He comes to the madman still dancing under the tree. He says, "Hey, Narada! Did you find out the answer to my question?" Narada says, "Yes, my son. You have to live as many lives as there are leaves on this tree." He says, "That is all? That is all for me? What a wonderful destiny I have. What a wonderful God. What love!" And a voice comes from above, "You are liberated this instant."

Look at this — the tragedy. The rishi has to live two more lives. He thinks it's too much, and therefore condemns himself perhaps to twenty more lives, two hundred more lives, we don't know. And this madman, who cannot even count five on his fingers says, "That is all?", and in that moment he is transformed. It is a question of acceptance.

If I think I am not afraid, I am not afraid. If I think I am strong, I am strong. If I think I am weak, I am the weakest. I only have to **think** I am rich to be rich. I don't have to **be** rich. Who is rich? Nobody is rich. We only possess money. We only possess wealth. We only possess houses, horses, cars. Can you say there is any really rich person? There are only persons possessing what they think are riches — some diamonds in their safe, some kilos of gold in the bank vaults, half a dozen cars, million dollar houses. What happens to all this? He is not rich. He is possessed by his riches. Like a woman is possessed by her beauty — she is not beautiful, she is possessed — it becomes the devil which is possessing her. A man is possessed by his riches. It becomes an obsession.

Let us free ourselves of these obsessive tendencies. Let us note that there is only one wealth, one wisdom, one beauty which we can carry with us — that is the beauty, the wisdom, and the wealth of the eternal which is inside me — the Self in me, which is eternally beautiful. It does not know age. It does not know sickness. "*Janma mrityu jaraa vyadhi.*" They say, the four *upaadhis* of existence. Birth — *janma*. If you take it, all the other three follow. *Mrityu, jara, vyadhi* — death, old age, sickness. One who is born will inevitably die. That is why the Gita says, "It is never born, and never dead." "*Na jaayate va mriyate*" — because one which is born, must die, even if it is a god. Therefore Arhatas have died. Rama died. Krishna died. One went into the Sarayu and destroyed himself in an act of ultimate despair for having sent his wife away, you see, after two *agni parikshas*. Krishna was hit on his big toe, right foot, by an archer's arrow, by a huntsman's arrow.

The Beauty of the Heart

So you see, that which is born must die. Naturally, it has to age, it has to face sickness. Therefore this craze for *mukti*. Why are people so fascinated by *mukti* even when they don't want *mukti*, when they don't want to die? Suppose we ask, "How many of you want to be liberated now?" How many people will say yes? Because we want *mukti* at a moment of our choosing. We do not know when we shall die. Like spirituality should be ideally commenced at the moment of conception, but since nobody knows when conception is taking place, it is not possible, therefore it is delayed to the eighteenth year, nobody knows when death is stalking him. To say, "No, no, wait, Yama! I am going to be liberated by my Master." And Yama laughs. He says, "Which Master? Have you a Master? Come. You are mine." *Mukti* not of our choice, but His choice. *Mukti* not at the time of our choosing, but of His choosing. All that we can do is to prepare ourselves for that moment, praying to Him, "Lord, at the moment of my death, may **you** come and lead me to the hereafter." Thank you.

A Child's Wonder
April 24, 1993

It is better to shine individually, isn't it? That is what we call genius. And such a person disregards society, disregards companions, and he goes straight ahead. Of course, there are moments of doubt, of frustration, but eventually everybody starts looking up to you. So there is this time gap which is the frustration. It can be shortened, if you are willing to achieve quickly. But then we delay and delay. "No, no, let me do it tomorrow. Let me do it tomorrow." So the gap is widening, until one day we are unable to make any more effort. We are too old. Then we say, "I was born like this. Let me die like this." That is the ultimate acceptance of the ultimate defeat. Isn't it?

So we must have the courage of conviction, that being in a herd, I cannot rise. Because the herd instinct is holding me tight. If I get out of this herd alone, I can make it. But then we have the problems of loneliness, of non-acceptance — people saying, "Oh, he's a useless fellow, you know. He is a loner." It is like that. So it requires a certain amount of courage. To be different always requires courage.

Now you are a girl. Everybody dresses in the same way — conformity. One comes dressed differently. There are jealous looks, there are snide remarks, all sorts of funny things, but — it may become the fashion. Isn't it? So the courage of conviction, that what I want to become, is **the** thing I want to become, is the only thing which is good to become. That's why I said the other day about 'being like papa.' Papa is a limited fellow. When we are children, it's good to be having a desire to be like the father and the mother, but we outgrow it when we come of age eight, nine, ten, eleven, twelve. By the time our girl is thirteen, I wonder how many of them really have any respect for their mothers. Now the whole problem is — how to hold love and respect together. That is why I said the parent, the leader, must always be ahead, so that you love and you also respect, because that guy is one step ahead of you all the time. If he falls behind and you have to look behind and say, "Where is my dad?" — love may be there, but no respect. So, respect we earn. Love, we feel naturally. So nobody needs to learn how to love. It is inherent in human nature. But to be respected, what has one to do? To earn the respect of others! To be admired, similarly, there must be something outstanding which others will admire. Beauty is not enough because it fades. Strength is not enough — it wanes. So what is that which will always be with us? The eternal thing in us. So we come to spiritual life.

That is the secret of the spiritual search. And when somebody very quickly passes through this material phase — why are these Westerners so eager in spirituality? — because they have seen to the limit the pleasures of money, the pleasures of the flesh, the pleasures of the palate. They are disgusted, and they say, "Come." There is no end to that. Also, today you can eat one ice cream, tomorrow again another ice cream. Today, if you eat two ice creams, you are going to be sick. Three? You will have nausea and vomit. Isn't it? So pleasure has a limit. Therefore we try to space out our pleasures. Then what happens? In between the two acts of pleasure there is an interregnum. What are we going to do with that? So there comes boredom, there comes frustration ... Knowing that is bad, we still want it today. Like the Americans — they

A Child's Wonder

want tomorrow's car today, and next year's pizza already here — things like that.

So the wise man says, "Even to enjoy, there must be the capacity to enjoy." And what is that capacity to enjoy? To take everything as a fresh experience — unique. The mango I am going to eat is unique. It should not be like the mango I ate last year, and say, "Oh, same mango." It's like that picture I saw about Nero the other day, you know, where Nero says, "It's all boredom," because everything is the same for him. The same beautiful girls dancing, the same wine, the same music, the same thing repeating ad nauseam, as they say. So even the best becomes nauseating.

So what is it that we can continue to enjoy without becoming nauseated? We understand that when we see that the pleasures of the senses nauseate. The mind is a little higher. The pleasures of the mind don't nauseate us. You can read and read and read and continue to read, without limit. Thinking, philosophizing. So, the subtler a thing becomes, the more enjoyable it becomes.

We have to learn this secret, you see, that in the gross manifestation of this world, there are always limits, and the limits are very low, very small. How much of pain can a man bear? How much of pleasure can we bear? It is even less. A man gets a lottery, he falls dead! He cannot support his happiness. So many people have died like that. It's not only pain. Pain never kills. It is disease which kills. What Dr. Mac said about pain being essential — not really. Pain is a warning system. I look upon pain as an alarm system which tells you that something is wrong — attend to it. But if I don't attend to it, then I am ignoring the alarm, like the car is being stolen, "Beep, beep, beep, beep..." the alarm is going, and we are still listening to the lecture.

Heart of the Lion

This afternoon I asked, "You know, in these malls you have hundreds of cars. If an alarm goes off, who is going to attend to it? So what is the fun of that alarm system?" Isn't it? Somebody will think, "Oh, somebody is opening his door. He will get in, close the door, and the alarm will switch itself off." So, an alarm system should **not** function, under ideal circumstances. You know, like the burglar alarms in all your houses — if it goes off at night, there will be a moment of fear. "What is happening? Who is entering?" So ideally, the alarm system should not function when there is nothing to be alarmed about. Isn't it?

So, in the perfect life, there can be no pain. Pain is for the frustrated individual, where he is doing things which he should not do, and pain comes to remind him, "Not this. Not this. Not this. Stay away." There is the famous instance of a runner called Primo Carnera, an Italian who died of bleeding because he was immune to pain. He was a marathon runner, and a nail went into his sole. He never knew it, because he had no pain. So, it is a warning system, it is an alarm system. Alarm systems are not necessary but, under ideal circumstances, they never function. Isn't it? "Oh, my alarm goes off every day. It's a beautiful alarm system." What is the use of such an alarm system?

Now, we talk of pain. Whether animals have pain is a moot question. They have babies, they don't seem to be in pain. We have read in novels like *The Good Earth*, you know, Pearl Buck's novel, how the Chinese women used to go into labour while they were tilling the field or harvesting. They went into a cottage, had their baby, and walked out again and started their work all over again. Today we need gynecologists, nurses, midwives, antibiotics, anesthetics. What happened to their pain? Because, in accepting child-

A Child's Wonder

birth as a natural thing, with love for the child which is being born, there was no pain. It was a momentary pain.

Well, I have pain when I swallow something, too, but I don't reject. "No, no, I don't want to eat anymore." I would be dead! Isn't it? There is the pain of digestion; there is the pain of circulation. What do I know about my inner pains — how my capillaries are responding, the veins are responding — 'gulug, gulug, gulug,' the heart is going on pumping. Have I ever asked my heart, "Are you happy?" Or my brain — so many electrical discharges going through it.

So you see, pain is not really necessary. Pain comes when we ignore the laws of life. Then pain is a warning system: "This is wrong. That is wrong. Correct it." Then it switches off. But now, in this modern age, we suppress pain by taking pain-killers. Now we don't know what is wrong. It's like you are switching off the burglar alarm when you are going to sleep at night, saying, "If the damn thing goes off, I will not be able to sleep properly." Many people are stupid enough to put off their telephones at night. Now, what is a telephone for? It is for communication, isn't it? Suppose somebody is very sick and they want to communicate. How will they communicate?

So if a man takes something to suppress his pain and goes to bed, he could be very sick inside, but he would not know. So, the warning system has to be open. We cannot shut it off. Yet it must not function. You understand? So pain is not so easy to understand, except by those who have undergone pain, and who know its necessity, who know its value, and who know, or have come to understand by proper living, that it is not necessary anymore to suffer, because that stage is past.

Also, the second aspect is, all our pain and all our pleasure is because of our samskaras. Why does someone like vanilla ice cream, and another chocolate chips? What is the difference? Why does one man like this girl, and another likes that girl. Isn't it? Given the same values. For instance, I don't like dirty currency notes. Something in me rebels. So I collect clean notes, knowing that they will be spent tomorrow, but while they are in my pocket, they should be clean. Some fastidiousness, you see — ridiculous! So, given the same intelligence, why does some person want to be a doctor, someone else a philosopher, someone else an artist? Why? The intelligence is the same. It is like one computer saying, "No, no, I will only have spreadsheets." Another computer says, "No, no, I love word processing." Computers cannot say it. So, my brain does not dictate what I shall be. The brain is the same brain. It can be used by an intelligent man for anything on which he applies his intelligence. Then why does this fellow choose to apply it here, and that fellow, there? My samskaras — they choose for me.

A good doctor is not a good doctor because he wanted to be a good doctor, but his samskaras forced him into being a doctor. Somebody's samskara forced him to be an engineer. A third one became an atomic scientist. A fourth one became a businessman. And we cannot say we chose. We did not choose. We were pushed into this.

I never chose to be a spiritual man or a preceptor. Mukund was saying that he did not want to be a preceptor. Neither did I! One day, Babuji called me. He gave me a sitting and started muttering something in Hindi. I opened my eyes. He said, "Close," so I closed. At the end of ten minutes, he said, "That's all." I said, "What were you saying in Hindi?" He said, "I gave you permission to be a preceptor." I said, "You

A Child's Wonder

never asked me. Don't you think you should have asked me?" He said, "Was it necessary I should ask you? In any case, you know, it was Lalaji's orders. Now, how can I tell the Master that I have to ask Parthasarathi?" (laughter) He used to put it in a very nice way! So you see, I was pushed into being a preceptor. I didn't really know what was happening. I thought he was giving me a sitting. And the next thing, I was appointed secretary of the Mission. And my father told me, "You know, you are getting deeper and deeper into this mess. One day this old fellow, (meaning Babuji), is going to put all his burden on your head and walk away." That's what happened! (laughter) My father knew long in advance. But I had no choice.

It is like a boy and a girl, very much in love. Is it any surprise that they get married? You cannot be in love and not get married. We are not of the Occidental culture, you see, where they pretend to be in love and don't get married. Because they want the way of escape. We don't want the way of escape. Who seeks the way of escape? Only one who is afraid. Isn't it? One who is afraid that this relationship may be a trap for me. But where there is no fear, what is the fear of commitment? Commitment is not really a commitment. I want to throw a new light on it — it is total lack of fear of what I am getting into. How can one walk into the den of a lion? One who is not afraid of lions, or of dens — one who is not afraid of death, who can go anywhere at any time — he is the fearless one. Isn't it?

[Child:] How do you overcome fear?

By loving the thing that you do so much. I have known young girls like you — suddenly in the family, at night, you know, the father is away traveling for his company or something. The mother falls sick and she has to go to the doctor.

Heart of the Lion

No telephone at home — you know, it is common in India. The doctor is three miles away. It is utterly dark. Dogs are barking in the streets. I mean, we don't have Sowetos in India, but there are enough dangers everywhere — imagined and un-imagined. But the girl, because of her love for the mother, doesn't think. She opens the door, walks out, and comes back with the doctor. Later on she wonders how she managed it. "How did I go at night? You know, I have never been able to go from this room to that room in the darkness without holding my mummy's hands. How could I go three miles and bring this doctor here?" Love removes fears. What I said from the Bible: "Perfect love casteth out fear." Love makes commitment possible. Commitment doesn't make love possible. "No, no. We shall love each other for eternity." That is a stupid commitment. In Hindi films you see it all the time. Not only in this life, but in the next. They are already creating problems for the next life!

So where there is love, there is commitment. Without love, there is no commitment. Whether you are a good doctor, or a good lawyer, or a good nurse, or a good scientist, your commitment is to yourself. We are all committed to ourselves. At least we think so. It may be a mistaken commitment. It may be a low level of commitment. "I am committed to my tastes." You know, as Mukund said. Somebody said, "I like to dress well." Why not? I also say it. It is a lesser level of commitment, because if I am going to depend on my dress for my respect, then I should do what Mulla Nasruddin did.

You know, the story of Mulla Nasruddin. He was invited to dinner by the Shah of Persia. He went, like Babuji Maharaj, in his old *dhoti* and pajama, or whatever it is. He was stopped at the gate. He said, "I have been invited for

A Child's Wonder

dinner," and they laughed at him. "Look at this fellow. Invited for dinner with the Shah-en-Shah. Is it possible?" So he went back, put on beautiful clothes, you know — all silk and lace and gold. Everybody bowed to him and ushered him in. He went to the table. The Shah had put him on his right, the position of importance, of dignity. He sat down, took off his coat, put it on the back of the chair, removed his resplendent turban, put it on the seat of the chair, and went away. The Shah said, "Where are you going? You are my most important invitee." He said, "Your highness, I was not invited. These clothes were invited. They will eat." (laughter)

Now, how does a man become simpler and simpler? Because he becomes more and more *in* himself, and does not need these props anymore. So, he can wander the streets naked and people don't see his nakedness. They see his grandeur, they see his nobility, they see his divinity, and prostrate before him.

So, love is the only commitment, and it is a commitment not made consciously. A mother does not say to the child at birth, "I commit myself to your welfare," or write a document. It is a commitment of love. Where there is love, the commitment is inevitable — you don't have to make it. Where a man says, "I am going to make a commitment," it is like the politician saying, "I am committed to the welfare of South Africa. I re-dedicate myself to the welfare of the people of this land, this great land, this holy land of ancient tradition, of lions and giraffes and zebras!" He forgets the human beings, you see! (laughter) In his love for language, flowery language, he forgets the human beings, but perhaps his inner conscience did not permit him to say it, because he has no commitment to the human beings. Because he doesn't love the people. He loves the animals better.

Heart of the Lion

I had a friend, a German works manager in my factory. One day we were driving, and he was driving very fast. A dog ran across. To avoid the dog, he swerved the car and almost ran over a human being. I said, "Mr. Scholl, you could have killed that man." He said, "I don't care. I love dog! To me, human being is pig, swine." He loves dogs more than human beings.

Today you see many people, you know, they are too much with their pets — their horses, their parrots, their rabbits. A child is dying across the street — they don't care. But they go and buy the most expensive dog food from the mall. Expensive television shows are shown about dog food and cat food. America is full of this trash. You see the American television — I believe about ten percent of the time it is going on advertising animal feeds! What has this society come to when we are not talking of human food, human values, human love, human creativity? "No, no, I am committed to the welfare of my pets. You see, poor things, they cannot speak. They cannot tell us what they need. We have to look after them." Yes, but you are ignoring the people who **are** telling you what they want, and what they cannot have. Why don't you look after that? "No, no, my dog never betrays me. You know, my neighbour — he betrayed me. My wife — she left me. My son has run away." "*Bismillah*!", you have to say, because there is no love.

The only commitment possible is where there is love. Without love, no commitment — then it is only duty, and duty is not a perfect commitment. Somebody gets a salary, he does his work well, and it is not so much a commitment to the work, as your own idea of your personal honour being involved. "No, no, I cannot leave my work undone." It is still a commitment to yourself — selfishness. "My work must be

A Child's Wonder

perfect. Everything I do must be nice." Who said so? The Gita says, "You have a right to work, but not to the fruit thereof." What does it mean? Good work or bad work — who are you to judge?

You know, there is a famous story, 'Shiva Kavi' in Tamil, where this Kavi, you know, is one who can sing the God into his presence. He becomes very arrogant. A horse is lying dead. He sings there, and the horse becomes alive. He is a Kali *upasaka* — devotee of Kali. The Lord says, "I must teach this fellow a lesson." So He comes as a Brahmin, and they are going together, they are eating together. When the host is not watching, the Brahmin takes a cup of gold, of diamonds, and puts it in his pocket and quietly slips out. Next they come into a house where the child is very beloved of the family. When they are not looking, he throws this baby into the well. Things like this. Then this Shiva Kavi finally says, "How can you do these things?" The Brahmin tells him, "You don't know what is going to happen afterwards. That baby was destined to die in the well, because if it had lived it would be a murderer."

You know, God knows — I don't know. I was telling Mukund a story of a vision I had. A very saintly ant, the saint among saints of the ants, is crossing the road, and the road-roller is coming. The ant is caught. It knows it is going to die. It is shouting, "Lord, Lord, why this for me? I am your saint. I am your devotee. Why this destiny of being crushed?" God smiles. "Because," he says, "you are going to be reborn a human being, with a better chance of evolution, you stupid thing!" Now, what appears good to us may be bad. What appears bad to us may be the real thing that is needed for us. Like when your mother tells you, "Sit down and study,

Heart of the Lion

Mukta," "What, this dirty mummy, you know. Study, study, study!" You understand?

So, when we don't have the wisdom of seeing anything but what is before our nose, as the English people say, we must hand ourselves over to somebody who can see farther. They are called seers. So, surrender is not denigrating myself or dissolving my individuality. It is just saying, "You can see better. Look for me. You can walk better. Carry me. You are stronger. Take my strength, too." So surrender is really entrusting ourselves to somebody, as we are, knowing that he will take us.

Like we get into a bus — I mean, it's not shameful for a man to go in a bus to Johannesburg. "No, no, I am a proud fellow. I have hunted lions in my time!" Yes, but that is in the forest, you know, when you walk four and a half miles and shoot a poor lion which has nothing to answer for. Can you walk thirty-six kilometres or sixty kilometres? You need a bus. Is it not surrendering to the bus?

So, surrender does not mean lack of self-respect or lack of the self, giving up the self. It doesn't mean anything like that. It means giving myself over to a higher entity, who can do for me what I cannot do for myself. Like when I go and lie flat on the surgeon's table — I cannot operate on myself, but he can.

And now, you see, this question of somebody getting, somebody not getting. We are always bothering — "Why this man became a millionaire and not me. Am I not as good? Am I not more pious? That fellow is a crook." But you see, something is taken away to make something, something is put into it to make something. You buy a cauliflower. You take away all the leaves and cut off the stem. Why? Why not cook the stem and the leaves? Then you put a little salt, and the leaves may be thinking, "For heaven's sake! Salt! He is ruining this! First he cuts me off. Now he puts salt, puts the whole thing in boiling water." Isn't it? But the maker knows what he has to take away and what to put in.

Like carving a sculpture — you cannot keep the rock intact. I always tell these fellows from Europe — nobody does anything. Nobody creates. You have a vision in your mind and you chip away all the extra rock, and the vision is there. You did not create that beauty. You removed the over-burden. Isn't it? And now, another artist would have done something else with that same piece of rock, because that rock has infinite possibilities. It only demands a person who can dream of a figure in it, and cut away the extra appendages. What else do you do when you carve something? You are only removing the surplus material which is obscuring the form behind it. "Oh, I created this sculpture." Nonsense. You chipped away a little rock and exposed the form that is already hidden within. You could expose only one form, whereas before you touched it, this piece of rock or marble had infinite forms in it. Isn't it? Can you deny that it had infinite forms in it? It could have been anything.

So we too, have the infinite possibility in us. But when we select with our greed, with our materialistic life, with our arrogance and our ego — "This I shall be." — we are limited into one form, and certainly not the best. Why do we call spiritual progress trans-formation? It is changing the whole thing. Making a beast into a beauty. How to do it? By knowing first, that I am on the wrong track. We all know it. We recognise it in our hearts. We know it when we are going to bed, that my day was not of the best — "I should not have done this and this and this. Lord, let me do better tomorrow. Let me change myself, transform myself." So you see, nobody can say, "I did not know." It is wrong. Everybody knows. Even a child knows when it commits a mistake. So it hides from its parents, who says, "Come here. What have you done?" Even the dog knows, because it skulks behind the sofa, into the darkness. And you say, "Reagan, what have you done? Come here!", and it's going under the chair again. "No Reagan." But it will not come out.

So it is wrong to say, "I did not know." We all know, but we do something else. Now, there comes our wilfulness. There comes our ignoring the inner call which says, "Don't." You say, "Oh, shut up. Shut up. Shut up." You keep knocking this fellow on the head, and he falls flat and says, "Okay. I am here eternally. You are not going to be here eternally. Call me when you need me." One day that becomes necessary, but I have forgotten how to get in touch with that fellow. The telephone line is cut; I don't know the number. So I need somebody — to awaken him within. Therefore Babuji said, "Awakening of the soul." It is asleep, because you don't need him. He has tried to poke his nose into your affairs occasionally, and you have just snubbed him and tapped him on the head like a dog — "Lie." The dog lies down. He is also asleep. Now I need somebody else to awaken him because I don't know how to do it.

So we need someone to awaken that which is asleep, and then to say, "I was wrong. You are right. Now you take over." So, I am only surrendering to myself, not to some misbegotten fellow called the guru. Who are you really surrendering to? To your higher nature. You are now ignoring the call of the **lower** and saying, "Shut up. He will speak now. He will walk. He will talk. He will do everything that is necessary. I don't exist." Then comes this beauty of transforma-

A Child's Wonder

tion, that everything becomes as if it was never there. The person changes overnight.

Buddha was a prince. You know the story of Gautama? He was a prince, the son of an emperor, married to a princess, with a baby. He had been living a protected life — arrogant, proud, everything — as a prince. He was forbidden to go out, because his father did not want him to see the miseries of this world. But one day he left, and he saw a man sick, hobbling, unable to walk. He saw an old man, grey hair, doddering around. He saw a corpse being carried on four able-bodied shoulders, and he asked his charioteer, the man who drives his coach, "What is this?" He said, "This is sickness. This is old age. This is death." Gautama said, "I did not know these things existed." The charioteer said, "But prince, you have been leading a protected life. This is the common lot of all human beings." Gautama said, "This I will not accept. Not for me is this destiny." Then he leaves his wife at night. To the sleeping wife and the sleeping baby he bids good-bye and walks away, never to return. And he becomes Gautama the Buddha — enlightened, followed by hundreds of thousands of people. Whereas, as a prince, he would have become a king. He would have been hated by all his subjects. But there, he would have slept on satin and silk, with all the perfumes in the world for him, in golden palaces, eating from golden dishes. Here, he was walking in the jungle, nothing on his feet, only a single covering on his body, but — the Master of millions. What is the difference?

So when we understand, that if the king walks on the streets without his crown, nobody recognises him. If the officer in the government comes out without his retinue behind him, nobody recognises him. We will understand, you see, that we are not recognised for what we are, but for what surrounds us — starting from our clothes, from our haircut, etc. So they say, "Enough of this nonsense!" Then you start to become something which people will love, adore, and follow. That is the transformation. Now they don't love you and adore you and follow you for what you can **give**, but for what you **are**. Therefore, the true personality which is adored is the Self. Let the Self shine. Why do insects come to the lamp when it is lit, as Babuji said. Why do the bees go for honey? Because honey is honey. If it was lime juice, they wouldn't go there. Isn't it?

So to attract, you must become that which is inexorably attractive — not just to the few, but to everyone. And this transformation comes. In the Upanishad they ask, "How to know this? How to find?" He says, "Just as the perfume of a distant flower is wafted on the breeze, and you just follow your nose, his qualities will shine before him. Follow those qualities and you will come to him."

You know, in the desert, animals can recognise the smell of water miles away. Bees go miles away to gather up their honey. Isn't it? So, how? Nature has given us the apparatus to sense that which we must sense, when we seek with our heart. Then the **heart** looks. The beacon of the heart shines. There is no darkness which can prevail over it. But we must follow that call! We ignore it. Mummy says, "No, no. First become a good doctor or a good engineer or a good politician. What is the hurry? First earn your two millions! Enough time to be a saint. You will start at fifty-five, when you have retired." But they forget that all the great saints were saints when they were in their teens — Dhruva, Markandeya, Nachiketas — name them, they were all young. The old only become foolish *rishis*, praying for power and long life.

A Child's Wonder

In youth we are idealistic. We follow ideas, not things. In old age, we are only suffering from the consequences of a life not well-lived, and hoping against hope that the door which opens when I am dead is not going to hell, but to heaven. This is the search of despair, the old record of despair. Every day is bringing *maranam* (death) nearer, Mukta. And this happens when you are around forty. Before that, nobody thinks of death. For a girl of fifteen, a man of thirty-five is old news. "Uncle, how old are you?" But when **you** near forty, and the wrinkles begin to appear, and all the deeds and mis-deeds appear before you — "What shall I do? 'Pit-pit-pit-pit,' this damn thing is going!" You go to a cardiologist. He says, "There's nothing wrong with you! Checked your blood pressure, nothing wrong." "Then what is this 'pit-pit-pit-pit' going here?" Alarm system! This is the big pain — the pain of the conscience — which says, "Beware! Correct. Even now, it is not too late." Physical pain is silly. This is the real pain — the pain of the heart. Heart-ache, we call it. The pain of separation, the pain of love lost, the pain of death of beloved ones. Why do people weep when a child dies, or even an old man dies? Because it is a separation, which perhaps will never come again together.

So spirituality says, "Bind that, in this life, now, before death intervenes, in such a way that even death cannot separate." You understand? Long answer to a small question! (laughter) But that is the way, you see. And in this process you will find the ego surfaces — who are you trying to impress? We all know barking dogs don't bite — it's a proverb. So the egoistic man, you know, people mock him after he leaves. But it cuts no ice. Whereas simplicity, you know — "Who is this fellow followed by twenty-seven people wherever he goes? Toothless man, bald head, wearing a funny cap, walking stick, and looking bewildered everywhere." Because everything is new for him. It is like the wonder in the eyes of a child — anything it sees is wonderful. Is wonder in the things that we see, or in the **way** in which we look at things?

If we are able to maintain that innocence of the child, everything is wonderful. To the child, even the dirty things — which older people call dirty — are wonderful. It wants to put its hand in its own urine, and 'tap-tap-tap' play with it, see the thing erupting out of that splash! "Oh, dirty child!" But it is wondering in its own creation, and says, "What is this which gives me so much pleasure? I splash it and it goes up dancing in the air, reflecting the sunlight." And we spoil that innocence by saying, "This is shit, this is urine." And if that child had wisdom, it would say, "But Mummy, what about that which is in my stomach? Is it dirty only after it comes out, or is it dirty even when it is there? What about the food I eat which becomes that shit in my intestines? Was it dirty before I ate it, too?"

You know, there is a beautiful story of a young man who wanted to be a disciple of a most famous guru — a very great, world-renowned guru. He went to him and said, "Lord, accept me as your disciple." He said, "*Guru dakshina*." The boy asked, "What do you want?" The guru said, "Bring me the worst thing in the world that you can find, as *guru dakshina*. Then I will accept you." So this fellow goes around looking for the worst thing, and you know, he cannot find it — "This is bad. That is bad. The black fellows are bad. No, no, there is this leper who is worse." Things like this, you know. Three years have passed. One day, he is sitting in the toilet. Suddenly, he thinks, "This is the worst damn thing. Nobody wants to touch it. Nobody wants to look at it. Nobody wants to smell it — forget eating it!", and he is

A Child's Wonder

going to grasp it, you know, to take it to his guru. A voice comes: "Halt! What are you doing with me?" He said, "My guru said, 'Find the worst thing in the world.' It has taken me three long years to know that this is the worst. So now I am going to take you to my guru as *guru dakshina*. It says, "Look. Yesterday, I was the apple, the pie, the beautiful papaya, which is not papaya of South Africa — the red thing. All this I was. You touched me, damn fool, and I have become this. Now, think for yourself, what is the worst thing in the world?" Then true knowledge, awakening comes. He washes his hands, goes empty-handed to the guru. The guru says, "Where is my *guru dakshina*? You have come without it?" He says, "Lord, I am your *guru dakshina*," and falls at his feet. "I am the most miserable thing in existence." The guru says, "Good. Get up, you are my disciple."

So you see, the worst is not outside us. The worst is inside us. When the worst is removed, the best is there. Isn't it? As Babuji said, "If you remove the saltiness from salt, what is left? It is no longer salt. If you remove the sweetness from sugar, what is left?" So, when all the qualities are removed from us, what is left? It is that which has no qualities, no form, no name — God. So, divinisation comes by removing things. I am arrogant — remove it. I am wise — remove it. I am capable — remove it. It does not mean we become incapable. On the contrary, we become more capable. Ice cannot come in through the chink under the door, but the wind can blow through it. Isn't it?

Subtler and subtler, you have access to everything in creation. Grosser and grosser, you are limited by everything. All this is grossness — wisdom is grossness; strength is grossness; power is grossness; ego is grossness; arrogance is grossness. So Babuji said, "Even wisdom we have to surrender." As Vivekananda says, "The intellect we need, but so far and no further." We come to the boundary, and then we respectfully bid it good-bye, because now we don't need intellect. If I am going into a territory where there is no north, no east, no south, no west, why do I need a compass? Where there is no wind, where there is no rain, where there is no sunshine, why do I need clothes? Isn't it? There is never hunger, never pain, so why do I need a body?

So, one by one these things are cast off. And then comes death — the divine moment when everything is God. And what remains? As Babuji said, "Remove all qualities one by one, and what remains is God." You understand?

So, long talk! Thank you. Thank you for everything, and look forward to our next meeting.